Apologetics and Social Justice

A Harmonious Call to Family

by

Dr. ant

Apologetics and Social Justice: A Harmonious Call to Family

Contents

Introduction

Behold, dear reader, in the midst of our intricate and tumultuous times, the voice of Catholic Social Justice calls, unwavering and steadfast. This tome endeavors to elaborate the noble principles tethered to Family, Community, and Participation, enshrined within the edifice of Catholic doctrine. In weaving this narrative, we shall traverse through philosophical discourse, sociological insights, and theological affirmations, that you may grasp the essence of a truly cohesive Catholic community, built upon the faithful bedrock of family and communal participation.

From the earliest epochs of human civilization, the family has been both the cradle of life and moral virtues. It stands as a sacred haven where one is nurtured, guided, and catechized in the principles of divine love and justice. In our exposition, we shall elevate the Family as the quintessential unit that germinates the seeds of communal solidarity and ethical responsibility. Together, let us delve into the sanctity of familial bonds, which, when fortified by faith, contribute indelibly to the fabric of society.

As we proceed, the formidable authority of the Catholic Church shall be contemplated. This authority, woven through the annals of history and substantiated by theological tenets, serves as both shepherd and sentinel. With its roots deep in Apostolic succession, the Church stands as the custodian of divine wisdom and moral guidance. Thus, we shall not only defend the ecclesiastical hierarchy but elucidate its indispensable role in fostering social justice and communal harmony.

The concept of Community, as propounded by the magisterium, transcends mere geographical or social aggregations. It embodies the very spirit of collective self-giving and mutual edification. Through active participation, each member is invited to rise above individualism and partake in the collective pursuit of the common good. Such a vision calls for an integration of one's faith into the civic sphere, transforming societal structures to mirror the divine order. Here, our endeavor shall be to illustrate how Catholic doctrine compels the faithful not merely to exist within society but to actively shape it.

Moreover, we shall bridge the realm of apologetics with the pursuit of social justice. The former, a robust defense of faith, becomes truly potent when harmonized with the latter's practical application. Envisage a world wherein doctrinal orthodoxy and ethical praxis walk hand in hand, thus fulfilling Christ's commandment to love one another as He loved us. In this confluence, the essence of Catholic apologetics finds its most profound expression in ardent social commitment.

Our discourse shall inevitably encounter the weighty challenges that oppose Catholic social justice, both from secular quarters and within the Church herself. Each criticism shall be faced with reasoned dialogue and evidentiary truth, fortifying the reader to contend with these critiques, both intellectually and spiritually.

Furthermore, through historical case studies and modern-day applications, we shall witness the transformative power of Catholic Social Action. Endeavors that reverberate through centuries shall stand testament to the enduring legacy and efficacy of the Church's mission in myriad contexts. This retrospective and contemporaneous analysis aims to inspire and galvanize the faithful towards emulation and novation.

In the twilight of our journey, we shall gaze upon the horizon, contemplating future trajectories for Catholic Social Justice and Apologetics. Emerging trends and impending challenges will be pondered, alongside a long-term vision for sustaining the principles of Family, Community, and Participation. Herein lies our hope, that the faithful may perpetuate this noble mission, ever adapting yet steadfast in its core values.

Peruse this literary endeavor, with a heart attuned to both contemplation and action. May we together illuminate the enduring relevance and profound wisdom encapsulated in Catholic teachings on Family, Community, and Participation, grounded firmly in the authority of the Catholic Church.

Chapter 1: Foundations of Catholic Social Justice

In the hallowed annals of Catholic tradition, the moral fabrics that underpin the notion of social justice are woven with threads of divine wisdom and ecclesiastical authority. This foundational precept beckons the faithful to envision a society wherein the sanctity of family, the communal bond, and the mandate to participate actively in the world's affairs converge into a singular, divine tapestry. As the flickering flame of Catholic teaching illuminates our path, it reveals that the cornerstone of social justice rests upon the twin pillars of familial harmony and communal solidarity. These are not mere abstract ideals but tangible, living doctrines that compel us to nurture our kin with love, embrace our neighbors with compassion, and partake in the divine choreography of communal life. The authoritative compass of the Church, hallowed by centuries of theological reflection, guides us to understand that the call to social justice is not an ephemeral whisper but a resonant clarion, echoing through the corridors of time and beckoning each soul to partake in the sacred dance of service, justice, and love.

Catholic Teachings on Family

Without the foundation of the family, the edifice of society would crumble as tinder before the flame. The family—enshrined in the sacred texts and rituals of the Catholic Church—stands as the primary and indispensable unit of both spiritual and social life. In the heart of family life, we find the intimate union of husband and wife, a holy covenant reflecting the bond between Christ and His Church. As one muses upon the essence of Catholic social justice, it is within the family that the principles of love, sacrifice, and the common good find their first and most compelling expression.

The Catechism of the Catholic Church asserts that the family is the "original cell of social life." This assertion places an unparalleled emphasis on family as a microcosm of the greater community, mirroring the interconnectedness and mutual dependence that God intended for His creation. As the seedbed of human formation, the family is the first school where virtues such as temperance, prudence, fortitude, and justice are cultivated. Within its confines, children learn to honor God, respect authority, and love their neighbors—all of which are cornerstones of any just society.

Familial bonds are not merely products of biological kinship but are spiritual kinships forged by divine command and sacramental grace. Herein, the Catholic Church teaches that the family is a "domestic church," a sanctuary where the faith is first professed and lived out in daily actions. This conception of the family is further illuminated by Pope St. John Paul II's writings, specifically his apostolic exhortation *Familiaris Consortio*, which outlines the roles of family members in their reciprocal duties to each other, their community, and to God.

Amidst the ever-changing tides of modernity, the Church's teaching on families remains a steadfast beacon. Families are called to reflect God's love through unity, fidelity, and open-heartedness. Parents bear the singular responsibility to nurture their children's faith, leading by example as stewards of God's love. This duty encompasses moral and spiritual education, encompassing the teachings of Christ and His Church.

The conjugal love between husband and wife assumes a sacramental dimension, signifying Christ's unbreakable love for His Church. This love, inherently unitive and procreative, is directed outward towards the welcoming of new life. In this way, the family becomes a fertile ground for the transmission of life and faith, each generation entrusted with the sacred duty to carry the torch of divine truth forward.

Moreover, the teachings on family life explore the roles and responsibilities of each family member. The Catholic Church posits that husbands and wives are co-creators with God in the act of procreation and are stewards of the family's spiritual and temporal well-being. Fathers are called to mirror God's paternal love through leadership marked by kindness and justice, while mothers embody our Lady's loving intercession, nurturing each family member with gentle strength.

This sacred vision of the family transcends mere ideals; it entails active engagement in the Church and society. Families are encouraged to partake in the sacramental life, especially through regular attendance at Mass and the frequent reception of the Eucharist. These practices fortify the family's spiritual fabric, enabling them to better serve one another and the wider community.

The Church's teachings on family also address the societal obligations of the household. The natural law, inscribed upon the human heart, calls families to be exemplars of charity and justice, to extend their resources and strengths in the service of those less fortunate. This outreach is not optional but a compelling aspect of living out the Gospel's call to love one's neighbor as oneself.

In this regard, Pope Francis has reiterated that the family has a crucial role in the evangelization of society. In his apostolic exhortation *Amoris Laetitia,* he stresses that families must be "salt of the earth and light of the world," embodying a love that is generous and life-giving. Here, the family's witness becomes a testament to the transformative power of divine grace, urging those around them to re-evaluate their own lives in light of eternal truths.

Furthermore, Catholic teachings do not shy away from addressing contemporary challenges faced by families. Issues such as divorce, cohabitation, and the redefinition of marriage present significant challenges to the Church's vision of family life. Yet, these challenges are met with pastoral sensitivity and doctrinal clarity, advising the faithful to adhere to the Church's timeless truths while extending compassion and understanding to those in imperfect situations.

In summation, the Catholic teachings on family within the broader framework of social justice present a comprehensive and integrative vision. The family is celebrated as the primary locus of love, faith formation, and societal contribution. Rooted in divine law and enlightened by Church doctrines, the teachings affirm the family's pivotal role in the realization of a just and loving society. These teachings, far from being archaic or irrelevant, provide profound wisdom and guidance for navigating the complex moral landscape of contemporary life.

As we ponder these truths, let us be reminded of the profound words: "As the family goes, so goes the nation, and so goes the whole world in which we live." These words encapsulate the immense responsibility and divine calling bestowed upon families. Through unwavering faith and steadfast love, families become not only the bedrock of society but also luminous beacons pointing toward the eternal joys of God's kingdom.

Community and Participation in Catholic Doctrine

Within the vast tapestry of Catholic Social Justice, we find woven a rich thread underscoring the collective essence of community and participation. These are no mere adjuncts but cardinal principles that unite us in a shared journey toward the Divine and through which the individual finds fuller expression in the collective. In Catholic teaching, community transcends mere social construct; it is imbued with a sacred significance, augmenting and elevating the human spirit toward spiritual oneness.

Let us venture, then, into the manifold ways in which the Catholic Doctrine elucidates the principles of community and participation. To speak of community is to invoke a vision wherein each person's dignity and worth are upheld, a realm where the common good prevails over individual self-interest. Yet, participation does not merely imply a passive presence but calls for active and conscientious engagement. Inherent in the very fabric of community is a summons to contribute, to share, and to partake fully in the collective life of the Church.

In the Ecclesial vision of the Church, the faithful are called to be vibrant members of this divine congregation. The Second Vatican Council expounded prolifically upon the notion of *communio*—a mystical notion of interlocking relationships, suffused with mutual love and sacrifice. Participation, within this context, denotes not only one's liturgical presence but the fuller involvement in the works of mercy, justice, and peace. Here, the lay faithful are not mere spectators but protagonists, bearing their own distinctive vocations and charisms.

Consider, if you will, the sacramental nature of the Church—an outward manifestation of inward grace. Baptism, the portal to the sacramental life, baptizes each into the community of believers. Each sacrament, an efficacious sign, fosters stronger bonds of faith and communal ties. Particularly, the Eucharist serves as the summit of communal participation, underscoring unity and shared spiritual nourishment. Such sacraments solidify the quintessence of the Church Community, binding the faithful in an ineffable spiritual symphony.

Participation, moreover, extends into the realm of social action. The Church envisions an active role for all believers in rectifying injustices, offering charity, and contributing to the commonweal. It is here that the clarion call to social justice reverberates most profoundly, urging all members to become architects of God's kingdom on Earth. Envision the works of myriad saints, whose lives illuminated the practical theology of community through their altruistic endeavors and zealous advocacy for the marginalized.

In broader terms, the social teaching of the Church, rooted in scriptural and patristic wisdom, enjoins us to recognize society as a field wherein divine commandments of love and justice are lived out. The late Pope John Paul II, in his encyclical *Solicitudo Rei Socialis*, posited that true development is not merely economic but fundamentally human. For genuine societal advancement, the marginalized and oppressed must be drawn into the fullness of communal participation, empowering them with dignity and opportunity.

Yet, let us turn our gaze not only upon the lofty heights of ecclesial documents but on the lived experiences of parish communities. Parishes serve as microcosms of the universal Church, fostering environments where communal bonds are nurtured and participation is tangible. It is in the local parish that the principles of Catholic Social Justice find their most immediate expression—through communal worship, social gatherings, and outreach initiatives.

The role of the laity cannot be overstated. With the advent of increased lay involvement post-Vatican II, the ethos of participation gained renewed vigor. Here, lay men and women are seen contributing not only within liturgical settings but extending their ministerial roles to spheres like catechesis, counseling, and social services. This egalitarian spirit denotes a participatory Church where each member, regardless of clerical status, is called to contribute to the great mandate of evangelization and social justice.

Perhaps, the communal dimension of Catholic doctrine finds a poignant expression in contemporary movements and conscientization efforts. Initiatives such as community-based participatory research—or CBPR—

underscore the empowering role of participation in effecting social change. This model, harmonious with Catholic tenets, insists on involving communities in identifying and solving their own issues, thereby fostering a spirit of communal ownership and justice.

Contemporary discourse on participation extends its tentacles into the realms of politics and civic duty. Here, Catholic Social Teaching invites the faithful to regard their civic engagement as an extension of their baptismal vocations. It's in the political and social arenas that Catholics are called to bear witness to Gospel values, advocating for policies that uphold the sanctity of life, economic justice, and the dignity of all people. Indeed, this active participation in worldly affairs elucidates the notion that faith without works is dead.

What, then, are the challenges to this utopian vision of community participation? The answer lies, partly, in the societal drift towards individualism. Today's culture often esteems self-sufficiency and personal achievement over communal reciprocity. Yet, the Church persistently offers a counter-narrative—a call back to the communal identity first exemplified by the early Christians in Acts of the Apostles, where they "held all things in common" and lived as a united body in Christ. This counter-cultural stance demands a reassessment of our own biases, prompting a reconsideration of what it means to live relationally and communally.

Additionally, the Church itself must navigate internal dynamics to foster true participation. Hierarchical structures, while vital, must facilitate rather than impede the active involvement of all members. Herein lies the critical role of synodality—an ecclesiastical process highlighting dialogue, discernment, and collective decision-making. Pope Francis has called for a "synodal Church," underscoring the importance of inclusive participation, not as a mere formality but as the very essence of living ecclesial communion.

As we strive to fulfill the Church's social doctrine, may we recall the words of St. Paul, who likened the Church to a single body with many parts, each indispensable and honored. This metaphor encapsulates the essence of community and participation: a harmonious entity, each part integral, contributing to the flourishing of the whole. It's only through such a robust, inclusive praxis that we can truly manifest the tenets of Catholic Social Justice, embodying a reflective, responsive, and responsible faith community.

In conclusion, the exhortation to community and participation within Catholic Doctrine is more than a theoretical construct. It's a lived reality, calling each individual to engage actively in the ecclesial and social realms. Whether through liturgical service, educational ministries, social activism, or civic involvement, the call to participation is a sacred duty, infusing the communal life with divine purpose and profound unity. Through embracing this call, the faithful can indeed transform society into a reflection of heavenly communion, a testament to the collective journey toward salvific love.

Chapter 2: The Authority of the Catholic Church

As the Lords of antiquity bequeathed their dominions to rightful heirs, so too did Christ bestow upon His Church an irrevocable authority, forging a divine lineage that transcends the mere annals of human history. This sacred mantle conferred upon the Church the unparalleled responsibility of shepherding the faithful, grounded not in ephemeral power but in eternal truth. The bedrock of this authority lies both in the apostolic succession that traces its venerable roots to St. Peter, the rock upon whom the Church is built, and in the palpable theological imperatives that underscore the papal office as an earthly manifestation of divine will. To question the Church's authority is to challenge the very fabric of Christian theology, which interweaves its teachings with the lived experiences and spiritual yearnings of the devout. Verily, it is through this authoritative guidance that the Catholic Church stands as the ark of salvation, offering a beacon of light amidst the tempests of secular reason and moral relativism.

Historical Basis of Church Authority

The authority of the Catholic Church finds its genesis in the early centuries of Christianity, establishing a foundation that would be unwavering through the shifting sands of time. As a tree's roots sink deep into the earth to anchor its towering form, so too does the Church's authority reach back into antiquity, drawing nourishment from the apostolic era. The linchpins of this authority are woven into the very fabric of ecclesiastical history, beginning with Christ's spoken word to His apostles and extending through the ages by the unbreakable chain of apostolic succession.

The nascent Church found itself defining authority even as it took shape. Jesus Christ, the cornerstone, conferred upon Peter the keys of the kingdom of heaven, uttering those momentous words: "And I tell you that you are Peter, and on this rock I will build my church, and the gates of Hades will not overcome it." Implicit in these words is divine authority, bestowed upon a mortal, thus establishing the bedrock upon which the Church would stand. This act of divine will was not mere symbolism but a consecration of leadership that would set forth an era of ecclesiastical governance rooted in divine mandate.

Thus, the mantle of authority passed first to Peter, and through him, to the bishops and popes who would succeed him. This apostolic succession is not merely historical but theological, for it encompasses the transmission of not just leadership but spiritual authority and doctrinal stewardship. It is within this continuum that the Catholic Church derives its unbroken line of ecclesiastical authority, an inheritance as sacred as it is historical.

Throughout the ensuing centuries, the establishment of ecclesiastical councils further solidified this foundation. The Council of Nicaea in A.D. 325 marked a pivotal moment, convened to address the Arian controversy, yet also to affirm the ecclesiastical hierarchy. Here, the Church demonstrated not only its authority but also its unity and capacity to preserve the orthodox teachings of the apostles. This consolidation underscored a critical aspect of church authority: the preservation and interpretation of divine revelation as handed down through tradition and scripture.

Intrinsic to this historical authority is the development and compilation of the Biblical canon. The Church Fathers, guided by the Holy Spirit, discerned and defined the books that constituted Holy Scripture. This task, undertaken with great care and veneration, further exemplified the Church's role as steward of divine truth. By the time of the Councils of Hippo (A.D. 393) and Carthage (A.D. 397), the canon of the New Testament was ratified, sealing the Church's role in safeguarding sacred texts.

The Middle Ages brought about a new epoch where the church's authority extended into the temporal realm. The investiture controversies and subsequent concordats, like the Concordat of Worms in 1122, underscored the Church's prerogative in the appointment of bishops, an assertion of ecclesiastical autonomy in the face of secular power. Despite the tumultuous relationship between the throne and the altar, the Church maintained its sacerdotal authority.

Another cornerstone of the Church's enduring authority is found within the writings and teachings of the Church Fathers. Noteworthy among these are Augustine of Hippo, whose works like "City of God" and "Confessions" delved deeply into the relationship between divine authority and human governance. It is in the wisdom of these patristic writings that we uncover a profound understanding of the Church's role as both shepherd and guide.

Significantly contributing to the historical basis of ecclesiastical authority is the role of monasticism. Figures such as St. Benedict of Nursia redefined religious life through their rule and order, cementing the Church's influence over spiritual and communal life. These monastic communities not only preserved knowledge through the long, dark corridors of the Middle Ages but also stood as beacons of ecclesial authority and moral rectitude.

Further enrichment of the Church's historical authority is seen in the legacies of councils such as Lateran, Trent, and Vatican. Each council, in its epoch, addressed doctrinal teachings and ecclesial disciplines, reiterating the Church's divinely conferred authority. The Council of Trent (1545-1563), in particular, robustly affirmed Catholic dogma in the face of the Protestant Reformation, articulating the integral role of both scripture and tradition.

The intertwining of Church and state in Christendom during medieval and early modern periods mustn't be overlooked. The political doctrine of the "two swords," proposed by Pope Gelasius I, delineates the spiritual authority of the pope and the temporal power of the emperor. This became a guiding principle throughout centuries, illustrating the Church's claim to authority in both the celestial and terrestrial realms.

As history strode onward into the Enlightenment and beyond, the Church faced burgeoning challenges to its authority. Yet, it adapted, drawing upon its robust historical foundation to address the emerging paradigms of reason and empiricism. The first Vatican Council (1869-1870) notably expounded the doctrine of Papal Infallibility, a reaffirmation of ecclesial authority amidst modern skepticism.

In light of contemporary times, the Second Vatican Council (1962-1965), or Vatican II, sought to address the rapidly changing world's challenges while reasserting the Church's foundational authority. This council embraced adaptation without surrendering the core precepts of ecclesial governance. It marked an era of aggiornamento, or bringing up to date, which reflected the Church's commitment to maintaining its historical foundation while engaging with modernity.

The Church's authority is thus a tapestry woven from the threads of apostolic succession, ecumenical councils, and patristic wisdom. These elements, collectively, form a cohesive whole that speaks to the perennial nature of the Church's role as custodian of divine truth. This authority has been acknowledged, challenged, defended, and reaffirmed through the aeons, providing a testament to its resilient and divinely ordained nature.

In light of these historical underpinnings, the Catholic Church stands as a bastion of continuity, its authority a beacon that has guided the faithful through the vicissitudes of history. It is a legacy carved not in the fleeting sands but in the bedrock of divine providence, venerable and hallowed across the centuries.

Theological Defense of Papal Authority

The Catholic Church, in its august grandeur and sacred history, asserts a theological foundation for the authority of the Pope that is rooted in divine revelation and tradition. This assertion is far from a mere hierarchical claim; it is a profound truth that has withstood the test of centuries, anchored in the words of Christ himself. When Our Lord proclaimed to Peter, "Thou art Peter, and upon this rock I will build my Church, and the gates of hell shall not prevail against it," He established an ecclesiastical bedrock that would endure until the end of time.

This Petrine doctrine, as it has come to be known, forms the very keystone of the theological defense of papal authority. St. Peter's preeminence among the apostles is not merely a matter of scriptural exegesis but is witnessed in the early Church's practice and acceptance. The primacy of Peter is preserved in the successive Bishops of Rome, who have borne the mantle of the pontificate with a charge that is spiritual and pastoral, embodying the unity of the Christian faithful. *Quod assumit, non dissolvit*—What Christ assumes, He does not dissolve.

The theological argument for papal authority is multifaceted, weaving together threads of scripture, tradition, and reason into a cohesive fabric. The Church Fathers, those illustrious doctors of the early Church, expounded upon this authority in their writings. Saint Augustine affirmed, "Rome has spoken; the cause is finished," signifying the finality and clarity brought by the pontifical decree. Cyprian of Carthage, too, spoke of the chair of Peter as the principal church from which priestly unity arises.

The Apostle Peter's unique mission is not an isolated honor but part of a divine design for ecclesial governance. The authority bestowed upon him, and his successors, is not autocratic but pastoral, a *servus servorum Dei*— a servant of the servants of God. This servant-leadership model is both humbling and exalted, as it mirrors the servant nature of Christ Himself, the shepherd who lays down His life for His sheep.

Varying in form but united in essence, the evidences of papal authority are scattered throughout the annals of ecclesiastical history. The Councils, both ecumenical and regional, have recognized the Bishop of Rome as a final arbiter in matters of doctrine and discipline. The First Vatican Council formally defined the infallibility of the Pope when speaking *ex cathedra*, adding a doctrinal weight to the longstanding belief in the unerring guidance of the Holy Spirit.

The theological defense is not solely retrospective; it addresses the contemporary Church's needs, reaffirming that the Pope's authority is vital for maintaining doctrinal purity and unity. In a world fraught with relativism and doctrinal confusion, the papal office stands as a beacon of divine truth and moral guidance. The Pope's encyclicals and apostolic exhortations continue to elucidate Catholic teaching, providing clarity in an often bewildering moral landscape.

Some may question whether such authority should reside in one man. Yet, human institutions lacking a unifying voice often succumb to division and schism. The Body of Christ, in its mystical complexity, requires a head— Christ, the invisible head, and the Pope, His visible vicar on earth. This dual reality does not diminish the authority of the bishops but rather enhances their ability to shepherd their own flocks in communion with the See of Peter.

Furthermore, the authority of the Pope is deeply intertwined with the sacramental life of the Church. The Pope, as the chief guardian of the sacraments, ensures their valid and licit administration across the globe. This sacramental stewardship is a cornerstone of Catholic life, touching the spiritual well-being of believers and preserving the Church's sanctity.

In theological terms, the Pope is often referred to as the *Pontifex Maximus* —the greatest bridge-builder. This title is not merely symbolic but deeply theological, for the Pope bridges the gap between God and His people, between heaven and earth. Through his teaching office, or *magisterium,* the Pope conveys divine truth in a way that is accessible and comprehensible to the faithful.

Additionally, the papal authority serves an essential role in the ecumenical mission of the Church. By fostering dialogues with other Christian denominations and world religions, the Pope seeks to fulfill Christ's prayer "that they may all be one." This unitive mission underscores the papal office's relational aspect, one that goes beyond mere governance to encompass dialogue and reconciliation.

Thus, the theological foundation of papal authority is constructed upon a divinely revealed truth, supported by scriptural testimony, bolstered by the writings of the Church Fathers, upheld by the ecumenical councils, and continually manifested in the Church's teaching and sacramental life. This authority is not an arbitrary imposition but a divinely-sanctioned instrument for guiding the faithful toward eternal salvation.

In defending the papal authority, one must also consider the mystical body of Christ. The Pope, as the visible head, complements Christ, the invisible head. Without the Pope, the Church would face a perilous fragmentation that threatens its universal mission. Through the Pope's universal jurisdiction, doctrinal unity and pastoral guidance remain intact, enabling the Church to fulfill her mission across diverse cultures and nations.

Through papal encyclicals and apostolic exhortations, the Church continually receives guidance on living out the gospel in a modern context. Theologies of social justice, family, and community life, find coherent expression under the papal direction, reminding the faithful of how to apply timeless truths in temporal circumstances.

One cannot overlook the role of the Holy Spirit in the theological defense of papal authority. The charism of infallibility, granted to the Pope when speaking *ex cathedra*, is a testament to the Spirit's unerring guidance. This gift is not for the glorification of the individual but for the preservation of truth, ensuring that the Church remains a pillar and bulwark of truth in a world prone to error.

In sum, the theological defense of papal authority offers a comprehensive understanding of the Pope's role as a divinely appointed shepherd, guiding the Church with wisdom and humility. This authority, deeply rooted in scripture, tradition, and the teaching office of the Church, remains indispensable for maintaining the unity and purity of Catholic doctrine and practice. In this divine economy, the Pope stands as the vigilant guardian of faith, a servant-leader, and a bridge-builder, ensuring that the Church, the mystical body of Christ, faithfully treads the path to salvation. Such is the sacred and unshakeable foundation upon which rests the enduring primacy of the Roman Pontiff.

Chapter 3: Call to Family in Catholic Apologetics

In the rich tapestry of Catholic apologetics, the call to family emerges as both cornerstone and sanctuary. This summons, echoing through sacred writ and tradition, compels the faithful to bind the domestic to the divine, viewing family not as mere kinship but as the embodiment of God's covenant with humanity. The family, in Catholic doctrinal eyes, becomes a miniature ecclesia, a nurturing ground where virtues are sown and faith deepened. Rooted in the scriptural archetypes of Abraham's lineage and the Holy Family, Catholics find in their domestic circles a reflection of celestial harmony. The apologetic endeavor thus links the sanctity of familial bonds with the overarching authority of the Church, creating a seamless garment where human love mirrors divine providence and unerring truth.

Scriptural Basis for Family

The sovereignty of the family, deeply rooted within the realms of Holy Scriptures, finds its genesis in the divine orchestration of human existence. The Book of Genesis provides an elucidating account wherein the Almighty fashioned man and woman, exorcising the solitude of Adam by crafting Eve from his rib. "It is not good that the man should be alone," thus spake the Lord, affirming the intertwined destiny of humanity through mutual companionship (Genesis 2:18). In this inaugural union, one perceives the primordial institution of family, ordained by God's will.

The Sacred Scriptures offer an abundant harvest of wisdom regarding the family. One must turn to the Decalogue, inscribed by the very finger of God upon the tablets of stone, where it is commanded: "Honor thy father and thy mother" (Exodus 20:12). This commandment, singular in its promise of longevity, underscores the essential role of familial respect and hierarchy. Thus, the fifth commandment stands as a testament to the sanctity and enduring significance of the family unit.

In the New Testament, our divine Saviour, Jesus Christ, sanctifies the family further through his own earthly sojourn. Born of the Virgin Mary and nurtured under the guardianship of Saint Joseph, the Holy Family of Nazareth reveals the sacredness imbued within familial bonds. The Gospel of Luke recounts how Jesus lived in obedience to His parents, growing in wisdom and stature (Luke 2:51-52). This narrative embodies the divine endorsement of familial allegiance and the virtue of filial piety.

The Apostle Paul, in his epistles, methodically delineates the roles and responsibilities that animate a Christian household. In his letter to the Ephesians, Paul exhorts: "Wives, submit yourselves unto your own husbands, as unto the Lord. For the husband is the head of the wife, even as Christ is the head of the church" (Ephesians 5:22-23). This exhortation is not a call to subjugation but to mutual respect and sacrificial love, reflecting the divine love Christ has for His Church. Husbands, too, are called to love their wives "even as Christ also loved the church, and gave himself for it" (Ephesians 5:25).

Paul's counsel extends to children and parents: "Children, obey your parents in the Lord: for this is right. Honour thy father and mother; which is the first commandment with promise; that it may be well with thee, and thou mayest live long on the earth" (Ephesians 6:1-3). Furthermore, fathers are admonished not to provoke their children to wrath but to bring them up "in the nurture and admonition of the Lord" (Ephesians 6:4). This symphony of affection and duty orchestrates a harmonious household, mirroring the divine order.

Embedded in the Old Testament is the illustration of family as a covenantal unit, integral to the collective identity of Israel. The covenant bestowed upon Abraham not only promised progeny as numerous as the stars but also mandated the transmission of faith and obedience through the generations (Genesis 17:7). The Shema, a central creed in Deuteronomy, commands: "And these words, which I command thee this day, shall be in thine heart: And thou shalt teach them diligently unto thy children" (Deuteronomy 6:6-7). This exhortation cements the family's role as the primary conduit of divine law and wisdom.

The Psalms and Proverbs, wisdom literature, abundantly celebrate the family and lay forth divine precepts for its fruitful flourishing. "Lo, children are a heritage of the Lord," states Psalm 127:3, illustrating that offspring are not merely progeny but divine gifts to be cherished. Proverbial admonitions, such as "Train up a child in the way he should go: and when he is old, he will not depart from it" (Proverbs 22:6), serve as perennial guides for familial devotion and moral upbringing.

The Prophet Malachi delivers an impassioned plea to uphold the sanctity of marriage and family, condemning faithlessness and exhorting fidelity (Malachi 2:14-16). This prophetic zeal underscores the divine expectation of familial piety and the sanctity of the marital covenant. Here, the eschatological vision intertwines with familial allegiance, waiting for the coming of the "messenger of the covenant" who shall refine and purify (Malachi 3:1-3).

The scriptural tapestry reveals the family as both a natural and supernatural institution, decreed by divine will and sustained through holy writ. It serves not merely as a social construct but a sacred covenant, rooted in the Creator's intent and fortified by Christ's exemplification and apostolic instruction. It is through this divinely ordered unit that human life finds its profound significance, identity, and mission.

In the Catholic apologetic context, the family is defended with vigour and reverence, drawing upon this rich scriptural foundation. It is through the family that the virtues of charity, patience, and humility are first nurtured, becoming the bedrock for communal and ecclesial life. The evangelistic mission of the Church, in turn, begins at the hearth, where faith is first sown and nurtured.

The family, consecrated by scriptural proclamation, emerges as the cradle of ecclesiastical and societal harmony. It is in these sacred bonds that the Church reads the signs of the times and interprets them in light of the Gospel. Thus, the family stands not merely as a private haven but as a public witness to the transformative power of divine love, weaving the very fabric of human society.

Role of Family in Catholic Tradition

In the grand tapestry of Catholic tradition, one thread is woven intricately:
the role of the family. The sacred unit of the family is consecrated, not
merely for the propagation of human life, but as a sanctified vessel for the
nurturing of virtues and the transmission of faith through generations.
Indeed, the family is the microcosm of the Church, a domestic sanctuary
where divine love is manifested in the daily acts of kindness, sacrifice,
and mutual support.

In Catholic apologetics, the family carries an indelible divine mandate.
Scripture implores us to glorify the union of husband and wife, likening it
to Christ's relationship with the Church. "And they twain shall be one
flesh" (Mark 10:8). This profound unity transcends mere companionship;
it is a spiritual communion, a minor Church within the Church, fostering a
sense of sacred togetherness.

The Council of Vatican II elucidates that the family is the "first and vital
cell of society". It serves as the primary arena for socialization, where
children first encounter love, respect for others, and ethical conduct. The
familial environment is foundational; devoid of it, society would falter
and the Church's mission would be significantly impaired.

The role of parents in this sacred trust is monumental. As the first
educators, they are tasked with the divine mission of catechesis, imparting
the faith not just in word but in deed. Life's first lessons in morality and
virtue are taught at home, wherein the spirit of the Gospels is lived out
through daily routines. This quotidian expression of faith ensures the
continuation of Catholic beliefs, sustaining the Church's influence in a
rapidly secularizing world.

A look into the annals of history provides us with rich examples, such as
the Holy Family of Nazareth. Reflecting on the life of Jesus, Mary, and
Joseph offers us a blueprint of divine family life. They lived humbly,
worked diligently, and honored the sanctity of their roles. Their example

underpins the significance of the family in preserving righteousness and devotion within the confines of the household.

Moreover, the role of the family in Catholic tradition cannot be disjoined from its influence within the larger community. The virtues cultivated within the family must extend to communal interactions, reinforcing the moral fiber of society. Families are not isolated units but cogs in the greater machinery of social harmony and mutual upliftment.

This brings us to the Sacrament of Matrimony, consecrating the union of husband and wife. It is a divine ordinance celebrating both the fecundity of human life and the fidelity of love. Marriage is more than a contract; it is a covenant witnessed by God, laying the foundation for the family as 'domus ecclesiae'—the Church in miniature. This sacrament fortifies couples to withstand the tempests of life, emphasizing that God's grace invigorates their union and family.

Into this sanctified space enters a profound responsibility to foster vocations. The family is the first seminary, nurturing potential priests, religious, and laity dedicated to a life of service. From this cauldron of love and faith rise individuals equipped to carry the Church's mission into the world, thereby amplifying its reach and effect.

In facing contemporary challenges, Catholic families must gird themselves with faith and resilience, recognizing their crucial role amidst a culture that often undermines traditional values. As society increasingly valorizes individualism and temporal success, the countercultural witness of a devout family stands as a beacon, steadfastly pointing towards eternal truths.

The writings of scholars and saints alike extol the family's sanctity. St. John Chrysostom expressed that "the household is a little Church", a refuge where God's love is palpable and transformative. Such reflections reinforce the importance of maintaining this role, realizing that the family operates as both a defensive bulwark and an offensive instrument in the propagation of faith.

Furthermore, the role of family in Catholic tradition extends into the economical and social teaching of the Church. Issues of social justice find their footing within the framework of the family. It is here that lessons in charity begin, teaching empathy, stewardship, and the preferential option for the poor. This, in turn, catalyzes broader social change as families live out and spread these teachings.

In the modern epoch, as we engage with an increasingly interconnected yet morally fragmented world, the importance of the Catholic family tradition grows ever more palpable. Technology and social changes transform lives rapidly, yet the family oriented toward Christ offers stability and continuity, a bastion of hope and spiritual resilience.

In conclusion, understand that the Catholic family holds loftier duties—not merely personal felicity but societal transformation through rootedness in faith. It's a divine calling that fuses the temporal and the spiritual, making it the fulcrum around which Catholic life pivots. As Saint Pope John Paul II poignantly stated, "As the family goes, so goes the nation and so goes the whole world in which we live".

Thus, let us treasure and nurture our families in the light of Catholic tradition, recognizing them as the hearths of divine love and truth. In doing so, we honor not just our immediate kin but also contribute to the edifice of the Church and the broader spectrum of human society.

Chapter 4: Family as a Foundation of Community

The family, as an entity divinely ordained, stands at the fulcrum of both ecclesial and societal life, a bulwark upon which the edifice of community is erected. As the seedbed of society, family life engenders virtues and molds characters, shaping souls in the crucible of shared experience and mutual love. This microcosm of community serves as the first school of social virtues, inculcating the principles of justice, mercy, and self-discipline. Through the familial bond, individuals learn to navigate the broader social order with a heart attuned to the common good. The family not merely founds but continually sustains the community through generational continuity and the rekindling of traditions that act as the cohesive glue of society. By fostering strong, faith-centered family units, one may mediate divine grace into the temporal realm, effectuating societal transformation rooted in the sublime tenets of Catholic doctrine. In laboring towards the sanctification of family life, the community itself is harmonized, and the collective participation in civic and ecclesiastical spheres reaches its zenith, forming a unified body that reflects the divine unity of the Holy Trinity.

Family Life as the Seedbed of Society

As rivers carve their paths through the land, shaping valleys and nourishing fields, so too does the family life etch its indelible mark upon the contours of society. The family, in its humble hearth, serves not merely as a domicile of kinship but as the crucible from whence the grand edifices of communities rise. It is within the quaint confines of familial life that the primal lessons of virtue are instilled, forming the bedrock upon which civilization stands upright and resilient.

Consider the anecdotal home, where a child first perceives the notions of love, duty, and sacrifice. It is there, amidst the seemingly mundane routines, that the young one's mind is framed and heart is sculpted. Through the rituals of daily life, the sanctity of trust and the inviolability of promises become apparent, setting a paradigm that reverberates beyond the homestead and into the annals of society at large. The father's stern yet loving discipline, the mother's unwavering compassion, these subtle yet profound interactions, form the initial alphabet of moral and social literacy.

Indeed, just as the steely oak springs forth from a modest acorn, communities are birthed from households teeming with life and virtue. Families, in their collective essence, act as the microcosms of greater human societies, each unit reflective of societal health and vigor. Where families thrive, one witnesses the flourishing of communal bonds, civic responsibility, and neighborly goodwill. Conversely, the erosion of family life portends a broader malaise, a fracturing of the social fabric that binds individuals in mutual respect and shared destiny.

To delve into the philosophical and theological substratum upon which this understanding rests, one need look no further than the revered teachings of the Church. The family, as posited in Catholic doctrine, serves as the 'domestic church', a sanctum where the laity first encounters the divine precepts and sacraments. This notion is not merely metaphorical but profoundly literal, enjoining families to become sanctified vessels through which God's grace flows into the larger community. Thus, the family serves a divine economy, uniting earthly life with celestial purpose, bestowing upon mundane existence an august sense of devotion and meaning.

In this grand scheme, the family's role as the seedbed of society is further accentuated by its inherent function in fostering intergenerational continuity. The transmission of cultural, ethical, and religious values from one generation to the next ensures not only the survival but the flourishing of communal identities. Grandparents impart tales of yore, parents enforce the venerable customs, and children absorb and eventually perpetuate these traditions, weaving an unbroken tapestry of shared heritage.

The societal ramifications of this familial transference are manifold. When families inculcate virtues such as honesty, fidelity, and compassion, these values become the common currency in the broader marketplace of human interaction. The young man, having learnt integrity at home, extends this virtue in his commercial dealings; the young woman, having seen her parents' dedication to service, brings the same commitment to her civic duties. Thus, the moral tenets nurtured in the cradle extend their influence, shaping the ethics and manners of the public sphere.

Moreover, the family acts as a bulwark against the prevailing winds of individualism and moral relativism that threaten to dismantle societal cohesion. In an era marred by ephemeral pleasures and fractured allegiances, the family stands as a testament to enduring commitments and collective welfare. It is in the intimate and often demanding spheres of family life that individuals learn to subordinate transient desires for the sake of enduring bonds and shared responsibilities. In doing so, they become citizens, not merely of a nation, but of a moral republic that transcends political boundaries.

One cannot overlook the psychological dimension of familial influence on societal well-being. The family structure provides emotional sustenance and psychological stability, granting individuals the resilience to navigate life's vicissitudes. The presence of a supportive and loving family acts as a fortress, shielding its members from the existential anxieties that modernity often exacerbates. This mental fortitude, imbibed within the family, equips individuals to contribute positively to the social milieu, fostering a community where the shadows of despair are dispelled by the light of shared hope and mutual support.

Furthermore, economic dimensions of family life warrant consideration. A family's role as an economic unit predates and indeed precipitates broader economic theorization. The arrangements of labor, the pooling of resources, and the equitable distribution of wealth within a family model small-scale economies that, when aggregated, form a stable and productive society. The lessons of thrift, industriousness, and generosity learned in the familial setting prepare individuals to engage robustly and ethically in the larger economic landscape.

Even in the realm of politics, the family exerts foundational influence. It is within the family that the concept of governance is first introduced and understood. Decisions made with collective consent, responsibilities allocated by mutual agreement, and conflicts resolved through patient dialogue serve as the embryonic stages of democratic participation. Herein, the family rehearses on a micro level what society practices on a macro level: the delicate balancing of authority and freedom, rights and duties, individual desires and collective good.

In sum, the family is an institution of unparalleled importance, sanctified by divine ordinance and validated by centuries of human experience. It is in the familial crucible that the virtues essential for societal flourishing are first forged, and it is from this primal forge that the robust pillars of community life emerge. Thus, to strengthen families is to fortify society's very foundations, ensuring that the grand edifice of human civilization stands firm and noble against the tempests of time.

Community Building through Family Units

In undertaking the profound examination of family units as the bedrock of community construction, we are summoned to traverse the annals of time and delve into the core of human existence where familial bonds lay the steadfast foundation. The family, in its essence, serves not merely as a biological entity but as a crucible of values, virtues, and verities. Within the sacred precincts of the household, individuals are nurtured, edifices of character are erected, and the fortresses of moral fortitude are fortified.

The symphony of family life, orchestrated with love, respect, and mutual edification, reverberates into the broader societal milieu, crafting a harmonious community. As Augustine might have cogitated, the unitary family functions as the seedbed, sowing the seeds of righteousness, fortitude, and fraternity which then flourish on the communal stage. It is within this microcosm that the first inklings of social responsibility and collective participation emerge, prefiguring the greater societal role each individual is destined to enact.

Moreover, when we contemplate the intricate interplay between family and community, the role of tradition and cultural transmission becomes pivotal. Each family, as a custodian of collective memory and perennial wisdom, imparts these treasured legacies unto its progeny. Thus, the family stands as a living repository of societal norms, ethical precepts, and cultural mores, making it a veritable bedrock of communal continuity and cohesion. Herein lies the teleological significance: families do not exist in isolation but are interwoven into the larger tapestry of human community, each contributing its unique thread to the fabric of society.

It is imperative to acknowledge that this role extends beyond the mere biological; the family as a spiritual and moral entity fosters an environment where each individual is called to partake in the larger communal vocation. The familial setting becomes a microcosm of the ecclesiastic community, nurturing the virtues of charity, humility, and justice. Parents, in their revered roles, are obligated to function as the primary educators of faith and morals, thereby enabling their offspring to grow not just in stature and wisdom but in grace and divine favor.

In the vista of Catholic social thought, the family is often portrayed as a "domestic church," a term which encapsulates both the sanctity and the social function of familial life. This conceptualization underscores that the family's influence extends to the broader ecclesial community, reinforcing the nucleus of Church teachings and cementing the cultural and spiritual edifice upon which larger human interactions are predicated. By fostering such virtues within the family, the community reaps the harvest of a populace imbued with the practice of love and service, which are the cornerstones of a just society.

Additionally, the practice of hospitality within the family marks a profound statement of community building. The act of welcoming others into one's home serves as a microcosm of the inclusivity and solidarity that ought to characterize the larger community. In this gesture, we find a living example of Christian charity, a tangible manifestation of the divine dictum to love one's neighbor as oneself. Consequently, such acts inspire communal bonds and mutual trust, which are indispensable to the fabric of society.

From the perspective of philosophers, familial relationships provide an invaluable laboratory for the contemplation of ethical principles and social virtues. Consider Aristotle's notion of the polis: the polis serves to perfect human relationships, a concept mirrored in the micro-polis of the family. It is within this intimate sphere that one learns the fundamental ethos of reciprocity, justice, and communal good. The relational dynamics experienced within the family unit, the commitments and sacrifices, mirror the duties and responsibilities expected in a well-ordered society.

One must also ponder the cooperative dimension of family life, which inherently promotes the principle of subsidiarity. Families operate through mutual support, with each member contributing according to their abilities and roles. This principle stands as a bulwark against the encroachment of centralized authority, ensuring that governance starts at the most immediate and effective levels. Consequently, in promoting strong family units, society upholds and safeguards the autonomy and dignity of smaller communities.

The theologian's prism reveals that family units provide indispensable formation for understanding the divine covenant. Just as God's covenantal relationship with humanity is marked by steadfast love and mutual commitment, so too is the familial covenant. This divine parallel impresses upon each member the profound responsibilities of fidelity, compassion, and sacrificial love. Understanding this divine mirroring further elucidates how family life becomes a prototype for broader communal structures.

In summation, if we were to envision society as a grand edifice, the cornerstone undoubtedly would be the family unit. The formation and nurturing within this microcosm of community life possess unquantifiable potential for the cultivation of a morally sound, spiritually enriched, and socially responsible populace. In its inherent capacity to educate, transmit culture, and instantiate divine virtues, the family stands unparalleled in its role in community building. May this hallowed institution continue to thrive and illuminate the path towards a more just and loving society.

Chapter 5: Participation in Church and Society

Verily, participation in the Church and society doth transcend mere attendance; it demandeth a zealous heart and dutiful spirit. In essence, 'tis the lay faithful's sacred privilege to interweave their existence with the ecclesial body, not as passive spectators but as active protagonists. Within this grand design, each soul is beckoned to embrace their civic duty and uphold social responsibility whilst grounded in the bedrock of their faith. Active engagement in the liturgical and communal life of the Church doth kindle a reciprocal relationship, wherein the faithful are enriched and the collective soul of the Church is fortified. Furthermore, such participation echoes into the civic realm, wherein virtue and charity manifest themselves through just actions and compassionate endeavors. Ultimately, this symbiotic dance betwixt the laity and the ecclesial society affirms the Church's role as a sustainer of moral and social order, ever guiding towards the common good, ensconced in divine love and everlasting truth.

Active Lay Participation in Church

In the grand tapestry of Christendom, the active participation of the laity serves not as mere decoration, but as threads essential to the very fabric of ecclesiastical life. To comprehend the significance of lay engagement, one must first appreciate the symbiotic relationship between clergy and laity within the Catholic Church. This relationship is neither hierarchical nor unilateral but rather an intricate dance of roles and responsibilities that culminate in a united spiritual mission.

To participate fully in the life of the Church is to embrace one's baptismal calling, recognizing it as a summons to devotion and action. From the time of the Apostles, the lay faithful have been integral in spreading the Gospel, catechizing the young, and serving in myriad ministries. Such a calling extends beyond the sanctuary and into the daily lives, workplaces, and homes of the faithful, where they are called to be the salt of the earth and the light of the world.

Indeed, the Second Vatican Council emphatically called for an enriched and expanded role for the laity, urging them to engage actively in liturgical functions, leadership roles, and community service. No longer are the faithful to be passive recipients, but vibrant participants who contribute to the Church's mission of sanctification, truth, and social justice. This renaissance of lay involvement is seen as a reawakening, reminiscent of the early Church where every baptized person understood their mission in the world.

Yet, this calling is not without its challenges. The modern layperson often faces a world beset with secular distractions and conflicting values, which makes their ecclesial duties all the more critical. A true manifestation of active participation demands a robust spiritual life, nurtured by the sacraments and sustained through continuous formation. To be effective servants, the laity must ground themselves in the Word and partake regularly in the Eucharist, the source and summit of Christian life. Such nourishment provides the strength needed to carry out their ecclesial missions with zeal and conviction.

The lay apostolate is rich and varied, spanning liturgical roles such as lectors, eucharistic ministers, and cantors, to catechetical endeavors, social justice initiatives, and administrative contributions. Laypersons also play crucial roles in councils and committees that help in parish governance and decision-making processes. These avenues of service empower the laity to take ownership of Church affairs, thereby fostering a communal and co-responsible Church.

An exemplary model of lay participation is seen in the various ecclesial movements and communities that have burgeoned over the past century. From the charismatic renewal to the Neocatechumenal Way, these movements serve as fertile ground for spiritual renewal and deeper involvement in church life. Their charisms enrich the Church and provide diverse pathways for the laity to live out their vocations effectively.

Beyond the church walls, the lay faithful are called to be apostles in the secular world. This is not a secondary mission but an essential extension of their ecclesial life. Each layperson, through their unique talents and professions, is equipped to infuse Christian values into society. Whether in the realm of politics, education, healthcare, or the arts, the laity are tasked with being leaven in the dough, bringing the Gospel to areas that clerics alone cannot penetrate. Their witness in daily life exemplifies the Incarnation, where the divine touches the human in the ordinariness of existence.

Moreover, the family itself becomes a domestic church, a vital arena for lay participation. Parents, as the first educators of their children, have the sacred duty to nurture faith within the home. This familial participation is foundational, as it shapes the future members of the larger ecclesial community. The family, animated by love and faith, becomes a beacon of hope and a microcosm of the Church's universal mission.

To further enhance lay participation, pastoral care must be adaptive and supportive. Clergy and lay leaders must work collaboratively, encouraging one another in their respective missions. This partnership is not merely functional but profoundly theological, reflecting the unity and diversity within the Body of Christ. Effective collaboration also mandates an inclusive approach, mindful of the gifts and needs of all members, regardless of age, gender, or social status. The Church must be a home where every layperson feels valued and called to contribute.

Lastly, education and ongoing formation are indispensable. The lay faithful must be equipped with sound doctrine, ethical clarity, and practical skills. Diocesan programs, retreats, and theological institutes play a crucial role in this continuous formation. When the laity are well-formed, they become more effective witnesses and agents of the Church's mission in the world.

In conclusion, active lay participation is not a mere adjunct to clerical ministry but a core element of the Church's life and mission. Through their varied roles and responsibilities, the laity breathe life into the Church and bear its mission into the world. The synergy of priestly, prophetic, and kingly roles shared among all the baptized ensures a vibrant, responsive, and dynamic Church, ever faithful to its Lord and poised to meet the needs of a complex world.

Civic Duty and Social Responsibility

As we traverse the venerable corridors of Catholic Social Justice and delve deeper into the tenets of Catholic teachings, we are inexorably led to a profound understanding of civic duty and social responsibility. These are not mere ephemeral notions to be entertained momentarily and then cast aside; rather, they are pillars upon which the edifice of society must be steadfastly erected. The moral obligations we shoulder are inexorably entwined with our faith, compelling us to act not solely for personal salvation but for the betterment of society as a whole.

It is in the teachings of the Church that we discern the imperative to engage actively in the civic realm, an engagement that is both a privilege and a duty. The exhortations of the Church Fathers, illuminated by the light of Sacred Scripture, bear witness to the necessity of participation in the fabric of society. They urge us not to retreat into cloisters of indifference but to step forth with a heart aflame with charity and justice.

Our civic responsibilities are multifaceted, encompassing a broad spectrum of actions and attitudes. From the casting of a vote to the defense of the voiceless, from advocating for the poor to safeguarding the sanctity of life, each action we take echoes the divine mandate to "love thy neighbor as thyself." Thus, our participation in civic life is a testament to our faith, a visible manifestation of the inner workings of grace.

Embedded within Catholic Social Teaching is the recognition of the intrinsic dignity of every human person, a dignity that demands respect and calls for justice. This recognition forms the bedrock of our social responsibilities. We are called to protect the rights of individuals, to fight against injustice, and to work tirelessly towards the common good. Each of these duties is not merely a secular obligation but a spiritual vocation, beckoning us to transcend ourselves for the love of God and neighbor.

In exercising our civic duties, we find ourselves engaging in acts of public virtue. This concept, deeply rooted in the philosophical traditions of the Church, urges us to foster a society where the virtues of prudence, justice, fortitude, and temperance prevail. Such a society is one where the common good is paramount, where the welfare of each individual is safeguarded within the tapestry of communal life. Herein lies the essence of social responsibility—a continuous endeavor to weave a social fabric that reflects the Kingdom of God.

One must not overlook the role of subsidiarity, a guiding principle in Catholic social doctrine, which advocates that matters ought to be handled by the smallest, lowest, or least centralized competent authority. By empowering local communities and smaller entities, we respect the autonomy and responsibility of individuals and groups. This principle enjoins us to support local initiatives and to ensure that higher authorities intervene only when necessary, thereby promoting a participatory and responsive civic life.

Furthermore, our engagement in society must be enlightened by the principle of solidarity. This principle reminds us that we are all interconnected and that our actions have ramifications that extend beyond our immediate surroundings. Solidarity calls us to recognize the bonds that unite us as one human family and to act with a preferential option for the poor and marginalized. In so doing, we become instruments of God's mercy and justice in a world often plagued by division and inequality.

In the realm of practical application, our civic duties manifest in myriad ways. Voting, for instance, is not merely a civic right but a moral obligation. It is through casting our vote that we participate in the governance of our society, striving to elect leaders who uphold moral values and promote the common good. Participation in local councils, volunteer work, and social advocacy are other avenues through which we can fulfill our civic responsibilities.

Moreover, the Church exhorts us to engage in the political sphere with integrity and prudence. Politics, often maligned and misunderstood, is a noble vocation when pursued with the intention of serving the common good. Catholics are called to be leaven in the political arena, bringing the light of the Gospel to bear on the issues of the day. Our voices must be raised in the public square, defending the sanctity of life, promoting social justice, and advocating for policies that reflect the moral teachings of the Church.

Incorporating a theological lens, it becomes evident that our civic duty and social responsibility are not solely grounded in humanistic ideals but are deeply rooted in our relationship with God. The commandments to love God and neighbor are inextricably linked, compelling us to act justly and love mercy. Our actions in the civic realm are an extension of our worship, a means by which we honor God through our care for His creation and our brothers and sisters.

The lives of saints and martyrs illumine our path, providing exemplary models of civic engagement and social responsibility. Saints such as Thomas More, who sacrificed his life for the sanctity of conscience and the rule of law, and Mother Teresa, who dedicated her life to serving the poorest of the poor, embody the essence of Catholic Social Teaching. Their lives testify to the transformative power of faith in action and inspire us to pursue justice and charity with unwavering resolve.

In conclusion, our civic duty and social responsibility are integral components of our faith, calling us to active participation in the life of society. Through our engagement, we bear witness to the Gospel and work towards the realization of the common good. As Catholics, we are summoned to be agents of change, to promote justice, and to ensure that the dignity of every person is upheld. In fulfilling our civic and social responsibilities, we not only contribute to the betterment of society but also advance the mission of the Church, bringing the light of Christ into the world.

Chapter 6: Harmonizing Apologetics and Social Justice

As the melody of faith intertwines with the symphony of action, we find the luminous intersection where doctrinal truths and social imperatives converge. This divine concord, far from being mere theoretical musings, demands the soulful engagement of both heart and mind. Apologetics, with its unwavering defense of ecclesiastical authority, must seamlessly merge with the palpable exigencies of social justice, lest we preach a faith devoid of works. Our sacred principles, rooted in the rich soil of tradition and scripture, must thus sprout forth practical deeds that bear witness to the love of Christ in a fractured world. Let not the chasm widen between theological verities and the clarion call to serve; rather, let our creed and conduct fuse into a harmonious testament that elevates both spirit and society. Herein lies the essence of our endeavor: to live out a faith that is both seen and unseen, tirelessly striving for a more just and compassionate world.

The Intersection of Doctrine and Practice

To traverse the expanse where doctrine and practice entwine is to discern the lifeblood of our shared faith in a most profound sense. Herein lies a delicate dance; the steps of doctrine, firm and unyielding, pair with the fluid grace of practice, responsive to the world's vicissitudes. This juncture—this fertile intersection—demands more than mere acknowledgment; it calls for a harmonization that speaks to the very soul of Catholic social justice and the apologetics defending the Church's magisterial authority.

At the heart of this synthesis lies the perennial tenets of the Church, whose foundations are as ancient as they are ever-relevant. The doctrine, a guiding star, illumines the path yet traveled, setting admirable aspirations for the faithful. We must not forget that these lofty ideals demand a tangible grounding in the realities of daily life. To practice these doctrines is to breathe life into them, rendering abstract principles into actionable deeds. This transformation, an alchemical process of sorts, is where doctrine finds its fullest expression in practice.

The interplay between faith and action is encapsulated in the virtue of charity, which stands as a testament to the harmonious balance we seek. Charity embodies the doctrine of love, elevating it from a mere ideal to a lived experience. It is in acts of charity that we encounter the Divine in the mundane, embodying the Church's teachings in a way that is both profound and accessible. To serve others with love is to mirror Christ's own ministry, wherein doctrine and practice become indistinguishable.

Moreover, the sacrament of the Eucharist acts as a fulcrum, balancing our doctrinal beliefs with the praxis of community life. The Eucharist transcends the mere observance of ritual; it flows into our interactions, compelling us to embody Christ's love in our relationships. In effect, the Eucharist serves as both a doctrinal anchor and a practical guidepost, directing our actions toward the realization of a just and compassionate society.

The ecclesiastical teachings on the 'Preferential Option for the Poor' further exemplify this dynamic. As a doctrine, it challenges us to view society through the lens of compassion and justice, urging us to prioritize the needs of the marginalized. Practically, this translates into direct action —advocacy, charitable endeavors, and systemic change. In this context, doctrine and practice do not merely coexist; they symbiotically enrich each other, rendering our faith both steadfast and dynamic.

In considering the family, the very cornerstone of Catholic social doctrine, we again encounter this confluence. The Church teaches that the family is the 'Domestic Church,' a living cell within the larger body of Christ. This sets the doctrinal stage, emphasizing the sanctity and centrality of family. Yet, it is through the lived experiences within family life—the nurturing of children, the mutual support of spouses, the embrace of elder generations—that these doctrines are brought into full relief.

Synodically, the concept of community participation draws us deeper into this intersection. Theological doctrines exhort us to be active participants in our parishes and civic spheres. This doctrinal mandate calls for a participatory approach to faith, urging the laity to take up roles that shape both ecclesiastical and societal landscapes. Here, doctrine and practice converge to forge a communion of believers united in their collective mission.

Let us reflect also on the prophetic voice of the Church in social justice. Here, the interweaving of doctrine and practice offers a powerful witness to the world. The Church's social doctrine, articulated through encyclicals and papal teachings, serves as a clarion call to action. These teachings demand a response, a lived commitment manifested in advocacy, service, and reform. It is in this response that the Church's authority finds its fullest expression, aligning doctrinal imperatives with practical initiatives.

This confluence is further enriched through the role of Catholic education. Catholic schools and catechetical programs are not mere purveyors of doctrinal knowledge; they are crucibles where doctrine and practice are melded. Through comprehensive education, individuals are equipped not only with an understanding of Catholic teachings but also with the moral and social frameworks to apply these teachings in everyday life. It is through education that the wisdom of the Church is handed down and put into action.

Yet, perhaps the most profound manifestation of this intersection lies in the Church's prophetic witness against systemic injustice. By steadfastly upholding doctrines that advocate for human dignity, the Church simultaneously calls for practical measures to confront inequality and oppression. This prophetic stance is not merely rhetorical; it compels us to acts of solidarity with those who suffer, thereby transforming doctrine into lived justice.

In conclusion, the intersection of doctrine and practice within the realm of Catholic social justice and apologetics is a dynamic and enriching continuum. It is here that the Church's teachings find their fullest expression, and it is through practice that these teachings become transformative. As we navigate this fertile ground, we are called to let our beliefs guide our actions, ever mindful that in this sacred interplay resides the true essence of our faith.

Balancing Theological Principles with Social Needs

The delicate dance between unwavering theological convictions and the ever-evolving tapestry of social needs is neither a modern conundrum nor a trivial endeavor. In truth, it is a pursuit as ancient as the Church itself. The harmonious convergence of these elements requires a deft hand and a heart attuned to the voice of both the sacred and the suffering. One must tread a path that respects divine commands while answering the cries of the human condition.

At the heart of this divine dance lies the imperative to marry the timeless truths of Catholic doctrine with the temporal demands of societal welfare. The Church, steadfast in its adherence to the eternal Word, nevertheless finds itself called to engage in the temporal realm, offering solace and solutions to the manifold trials of humanity. Herein lies a principle central to Catholic social teaching: the innate dignity of every human being, a concept rooted in theological precepts yet proclaimed in the public square.

Such dignity, derived from mankind being created imago Dei, necessitates the Church's active role in addressing societal issues. The push to balance theology with social needs compels us to look deeply into scriptural exegesis, reconciled with a palpable compassion that knows no borders. This theological underpinning is not an abstract exercise; it demands concrete action, manifesting in feeding the hungry, sheltering the homeless, and advocating for the oppressed.

The notion of caritas, or charity, finds its completion in justice. While charity addresses immediate needs with benevolent hands, justice seeks to restructure societies in ways that those needs may diminish. It is here the theological principles of the Church act as both guide and boundary. We are exhorted to mold our communities in the likeness of God's Kingdom, a realm where love and equity prevail. However, the pursuit of social justice must not contravene the teachings handed down through the ages.

Consider the Church's stance on life issues. Upholding life from conception to natural death is more than a theological principle; it is a mandate shaping the Church's approach to social needs. The sanctity of life informs comprehensive stances on issues like abortion, euthanasia, and even the death penalty. The challenge, then, is integrating these doctrines into a society increasingly swayed by relativism and utilitarian ethics. This integration demands robust apologetics, defending the faith's stances while demonstrating their inherent regard for human dignity.

In a secular world often beset by moral vacillations, the Church's unwavering adherence to certain principles can seem out of step. Yet this steadfastness is precisely what grants the Church its transcendent authority and moral clarity. For instance, the Church's teachings on family as the fundamental unit of society inform its social justice initiatives. Family stability promotes societal stability, embodying both theological and social imperatives.

Yet, the focus must broaden beyond the family to embrace community and participation. The principle of subsidiarity, deeply rooted in Catholic social teaching, posits that matters ought to be handled by the smallest, lowest, or least centralized competent authority. This principle is essential when crafting responses to social needs, ensuring that solutions are not only theologically sound but also practically effective. Here, the Church becomes a vibrant participant in social life, ever mindful of its doctrinal boundaries.

The principle of solidarity further underpins the Church's engagement with social justice. Solidarity speaks to our interconnectedness, our shared humanity, and the communal nature of our salvation. Theologically, this aligns with the doctrine of the Mystical Body of Christ —wherein the joys and sufferings of one part affect the whole. Practically, solidarity propels us to stand alongside those marginalized by poverty, exploitation, or discrimination.

In merging theological principles with social action, the challenge often lies in application rather than theory. For instance, Catholic social teaching advocates for the preferential option for the poor, a principle calling for heightened focus on the needs of the most vulnerable. This calls for nuanced approaches that are vigilant of unintended consequences while remaining firmly rooted in doctrinal tenets.

Time and again, the Church must discern and navigate modern issues that lack direct scriptural reference. These challenges necessitate a dynamic understanding and application of timeless principles, always infused with prudence and pastoral sensitivity. As new social issues emerge—be they technological advancements affecting labor or policies impacting immigration—the Church must offer responses anchored firmly in eternal truths yet responsive to contemporary conditions.

Ultimately, the task of balancing theological principles with social needs requires both an unyielding grasp on the divine and a compassionate touch upon the earthly. This paradox is embodied in the very Incarnation—God becoming man, the eternal Word entering time and space. In this mystery, we find our model for engaging the world: to be in it, but not of it, ever upholding divine wisdom while ceaselessly laboring for the common good.

Such a balance is neither static nor absolute; it is a continual, dynamic endeavor, requiring vigilance and reverence. It must eschew both rigid dogmatism that ignores human suffering and a facile liberalism that compromises core beliefs. Hence, the Church proclaims the inviolability of marriage while tending to those broken by its failures, it asserts the sanctity of life while ministering to those who suffer from its neglect, and it never ceases from articulating these truths with a compelling love that seeks not only to comfort but also to challenge and to convert.

Thus, the marriage of theology and social action within the Catholic tradition is characterized by a delicate equilibrium—a perennial tension that must be navigated with fidelity, wisdom, and love. It is a balance that continually turns to the light of Scripture, Tradition, and the lived witness of the saints, even as it engages the pressing needs and challenges of contemporary social life.

Chapter 7: Case Studies in Catholic Social Action

In the grand tapestry of human endeavor, one finds threads woven by devout souls who, impelled by love and justice, have translated Catholic teachings into tangible deeds. Witness the luminous chronicles of ages past, where family-centered initiatives not only nurtured the hearth but fortified the streets of an entire polity. Indelibly remembered are the charitable vocations of St. Vincent de Paul and the pioneering educational reforms of St. John Bosco, whose ministries were beacons of hope in times of despair. Now, in contemporary parish communities, these virtues are mirrored in programs that range from holistic family support services to the invigorating praxis of community gardens. In these havens, the principles of subsidiarity and solidarity blossom, as individuals gather, not merely as parishioners, but as active co-laborers in the vineyard of communal salvation. Each case etched therein exemplifies a praxis replete with dynamism, continuously evolving to meet the exigencies of a modern world, yet steadfastly rooted in the immutable truths of the Church.

Historical Examples of Family-Centered Initiatives

In yesteryears, the Catholic Church's dogged allegiance to family-centered initiatives was not so much a goal but a calling—a divine ordination of sorts. One may reflect upon the medieval period wherein the sanctity of family life was inextricably linked with the ecclesiastical domain. The very edicts and doctrines stemming from the esteemed councils of the Church reverberated through the cobbled streets and rustic countrysides, echoing the imperative of family as the cornerstone of both faith and community.

Consider the times of the early Apostolic Fathers, where in the nascent Christian communities, the family was perceived as a "domestic church." It was within these humble abodes that the faith was not merely practiced but lived, taught, and handed down. The Didache, one of the earliest Christian writings, instructed the faithful on matters of catechesis, moral teachings, and communal living, which naturally emanated from the core of family life. Every hearth became a sacred altar, every family meal a Eucharistic celebration, imbued with an almost sacramental significance.

Transitioning to the medieval era, the sanctity of marriage and the family was further enshrined by the edicts of the Fourth Lateran Council in 1215 AD. Here, the Church codified practices that underscored the indelible bond of marriage, emphasizing the sacramental nature of familial ties. Marriages were to be publicly proclaimed, and children were to be viewed not merely as progeny but as souls to be nurtured in the faith. The Council asserted the necessity of conjugal fidelity and the sacred duty of progeny rearing in alignment with Christ's teachings.

During the age of the Renaissance, one cannot overlook the influential role of Catholic sodalities and confraternities. These were lay groups that took upon themselves the mantle of social and spiritual welfare, extending their pious works into the quotidian matters of family existence. The Confraternity of the Blessed Sacrament, originating in 16th-century Italy, epitomized the Church's endeavors to nourish family life. Members engaged in acts that ameliorated the woes of impoverishment, providing sustenance and spiritual solace to struggling families—thereby knitting a fabric of divine charity and tangible support.

Another luminous example emerges from the annals of the Counter-Reformation, where under the aegis of the Council of Trent (1545-1563), the Church fathers exhorted the robust catechesis of children within the family setting. Catechisms were disseminated with fervor, and the Tridentine decrees saw to it that educational endeavours were not only clerical but familial responsibilities. The Christian Doctrine Confraternities (Confraternities of Christian Doctrine, or CCD) became instrumental in shaping the spiritual formation of youth, exemplifying the Church's unwavering commitment to nurturing the faith from the familial root.

In more recent centuries, consider the Catholic Social Encyclicals of the 19th and 20th centuries, such as Pope Leo XIII's "Rerum Novarum" (1891) and Pope Pius XI's "Quadragesimo Anno" (1931). These encyclicals provided a theological and moral compass for the faithful, particularly amidst the upheavals of industrialization. The family unit was championed as the bedrock upon which social order was to be constructed, and the pontiffs ardently sought to protect families from the depredations of exploitative labor systems.

During the dire days of the Great Depression, the establishment of the Catholic Worker Movement by Dorothy Day and Peter Maurin in 1933 further illuminated the Church's mission to support and sustain families. Their houses of hospitality were sanctuaries for the destitute, embodying the corporal works of mercy that had been professed for centuries. Here, the family was not merely a biological construct but an inclusive community born of necessity and grace, revealing a living testament to the magisterium of Catholic Social Teaching.

In juxtaposition, the aftermath of World War II saw the emergence of the Family Rosary Crusade spearheaded by Servant of God Father Patrick Peyton. His adage, "The family that prays together stays together," resonates through the corridors of history. The initiative galvanized millions, rekindling the spirit of familial devotion and collective prayer, suggesting that in unity and faith, the family possesses immense fortitude and divine favor.

Moreover, one cannot overlook the significance of "Familiaris Consortio," the Apostolic Exhortation penned by Pope John Paul II in 1981. This seminal document expounds on the role of the Christian family in the modern world. The Pope delineated the multifarious roles of family life - as a community of persons, a sanctuary for the upbringing of children, and a bulwark against societal disintegration. His exhortation was both a consoling pastoral reminder and a clarion call to recognize the profound ecclesial and societal implications of nurturing steadfast familial bonds.

It is in the panoramic sweep of history that we find countless other instances where the Church has vigilantly guarded the sanctity of familial life. The Pontifical Council for the Family, established by Pope John Paul II in 1981, has been steadfast in its advocacy and support for familial structures. Be it through papal encyclicals, synods, or grassroots initiatives, the Church's unwavering support for family-centric actions remains palpably evident.

As one traverses through these historical examples, a tapestry of divine-human collaboration unfurls, wherein the family is ever the locus of spiritual and communal integrity. These family-centered initiatives are luminous waypoints, guiding the Church's unending pilgrimage towards justice, love, and societal harmony. The family, as evinced in these initiatives, remains the first school of virtue, the primary field of social endeavor, and the invincible fortress of faith.

Modern Applications in Parish Communities

In the symphony of Catholic social justice, the parish stands as a luminous beacon. It is within these sacred communal spheres that the principles of family, community, and participation materialize into living testimony. The transcendence of doctrine into daily life in parish communities showcases how profoundly Catholic teachings can nurture and transform society today. Let us embark then into an exploration of these modern applications, wherein the tenets of the Church enliven the heart of community.

Today's parishes serve not just as places of worship but as vibrant epicenters of social action. The weekly Mass, with its solemn liturgy and sacred rituals, is but the overture. Beyond the ceremonial rites, parishes embody a commitment to the social teachings of the Church through multifaceted programs that address the temporal needs of their members and the broader community. Initiatives like food pantries, healthcare clinics, and educational forums are profound examples of how modern parishes adapt to meet contemporary social challenges.

Crucially, these applications are not mere acts of charity but incarnations of a deeper theological mandate. They birth from the Gospel's call to love thy neighbor as thyself, echoing Christ's directive to care for "the least of these." By integrating such services into parish life, the Church ensures that its social justice mission is not relegated to the abstract but is rooted in tangible actions. This blend of faith and works is an undeniable expression of the ecclesial body fulfilling its divine commission.

At the forefront of these modern ventures lie ministries tailored to fortify families—the building blocks of society. Parish-led marriage preparation courses, parenting workshops, and youth ministries are designed to support familial unity and spiritual growth. These resources are vital in navigating the complexities of the modern age, offering guidance and solidarity grounded in centuries-old wisdom. The family, being the "domestic church," receives holistic nurturing in an environment that honors both its spiritual and worldly aspects.

Moreover, the parishes are innovators in fostering community participation. Encouraging active lay involvement stands as a testament to the Church's recognition of each member's unique gifts and call to service. From liturgical roles such as lectors and choir members to administrative duties on parish councils, laypersons find myriad avenues to contribute meaningfully. This participatory culture underlines the ecclesiology of the Church—a communal body where every part plays a crucial role.

One can observe further blossoming of these principles through outreach innovations like JustFaith groups, where parishioners engage in structured programs of education and action focused on social justice. These groups often delve into issues such as poverty, racism, and ecological sustainability, providing parishioners with both the theological framework and practical tools to effect change. The synthesis of learning and action in such settings equips the faithful to address systemic injustices, making the Church a proactive force for societal betterment.

Equally significant are the parish initiatives aimed at ecological stewardship, reflecting Pope Francis' call in *Laudato Si'*. Community gardens, recycling programs, and educational campaigns on environmental responsibility illustrate modern parishes' commitment to this call. These activities not only foster a sense of communal purpose but also manifest a deeply theological appreciation for creation, reinforcing the interconnectedness of all life.

Interfaith collaborations represent another remarkable application within contemporary parish communities. By building alliances with other religious and civic organizations, Catholic parishes expand their reach and impact. These partnerships often lead to joint ventures such as interfaith dialogues, service projects, and advocacy efforts. Through such solidarity, parishes exemplify the Catholic commitment to unity within diversity, boldly witnessing to the universality of God's love.

Furthermore, technological advancements provide new modalities for pastoral care and outreach. Many parishes have embraced digital platforms to enhance connectivity and engagement. Online streaming of Mass, virtual faith formation classes, and social media outreach campaigns ensure that the Church's message and ministry are accessible to all, especially the homebound and those on society's margins. These digital strategies preserve the sense of belonging and participation that underpin parish life.

In this extensive tableau, the collaboration between clergy and laity emerges as a pillar of effective application. The pastoral leadership, imbued with theological and spiritual acumen, harnesses the diverse talents and resources of the laity. Together, they navigate the myriad needs of contemporary society with creativity and a shared sense of mission. This ecclesial synergy exemplifies the dynamic interplay of ordination and baptismal priesthood envisioned by Vatican II.

Then there are the parish schools and religious education programs that stand as enduring beacons of Catholic identity and social teaching. These institutions do more than impart academic knowledge; they inculcate values of justice, service, and community. By grooming the young to be conscientious and compassionate citizens, parishes sow seeds for a more equitable and harmonious society.

However, these modern applications face their own share of challenges. Cultural secularization, economic constraints, and internal governance issues can threaten the vibrancy of parish initiatives. Yet, within these trials lie opportunities for resilience and renewal. The adaptability of parish communities in the face of such challenges mirrors the Church's broader journey through history, where renewal often springs from adversity.

In recognizing these modern applications, one must also acknowledge the lived experiences of parishioners. It is through their testimonies that the profound impact of parish initiatives becomes most evident. The single mother aided by the parish food pantry, the immigrant family finding solace in a supportive community, the teenager discovering faith and purpose through youth ministry—all these stories reflect the transformative power of parishes grounded in Catholic social teaching.

Thus, in conclusion, modern parishes stand as dynamic epitomes of the Church's call to social action rooted in family and community. Through a myriad of innovative and compassionate initiatives, they manifest the enduring relevance of Catholic social justice principles. In translating doctrine into practice, these parish communities not only uplift their members but also bear witness to the eternal truth of the Gospel in an ever-changing world.

Chapter 8: Philosophical Perspectives on Family and Authority

Navigating the intricate landscape of family and authority, one discovers the profound interlocking of roles and responsibilities, elevated through Catholic philosophy. Herein lies the kernel of communal harmony and divine hierarchy, a delicate equilibrium manifesting in familial constructs and ecclesiastical realms. Philosophers across epochs have bestowed upon us a treasury of wisdom, dissecting the sinews that bind authority with moral duty. The profound musings of these erudite thinkers breathe life into the Catholic doctrine, weaving theological threads with sociological and psychological insights. This synthesis does more than illuminate; it fortifies the sacred edifice of family as the cornerstone of both society and salvation, upholding not mere tradition but a sanctified order ordained by the Almighty Himself. Thus, the nexus of family and authority emerges not as an arbitrary construct but as a divine tapestry woven with intent and reverence, inviting us to ponder, "What is the good life?" in the light of eternal truth.

Contributions of Philosophers to Catholic Thought

The annals of philosophic jurisprudence and theology brim with luminaries whose cogitations have indelibly influenced Catholic thought, forming a fertile communion between reason and faith. Their contemplations on family and authority have woven a rich tapestry of wisdom, elucidating the profound synthesis inherent in the Church's teachings. In scrutinizing the myriad contributions of these philosophers, we glean the thread that binds human existence to divine precepts, offering a panoply of insights into the intricate relationship between the family unit and ecclesiastical authority.

Consider, if thou wilt, the magisterial musings of Saint Augustine. His musings on the City of God and the earthly city delineate a vision where the family stands as a microcosm of spiritual communion. Augustine posited that familial relationships model the Trinitarian love, echoing the relationality inherent in the divine substance. In his confessions and treatises, he implored the faithful to regard the household as the primary locus of moral formation, instrumental in promulgating the virtues that underpin communal life. His discourse on the primacy of caritas—love—emanates as a beacon for the sanctity of familial bonds, reinforcing the ecclesiastical dictum that the family is the domestic church.

Conversely, the rational rigor of Thomas Aquinas bequeaths a formidable edifice upon which Catholic thought stands. His synthesis of Aristotelian philosophy with Christian doctrine showcased a harmonization wherein reason serves not as an antagonist to faith, but as its handmaiden. In Aquinas' Summa Theologica, we witness the articulation of natural law—a principle asserting that human reason discerns moral imperatives imbued by the Creator. He argued that the family is a natural society with its own inherent rights and responsibilities, derived from God's eternal law. Aquinas' elucidation of parental authority and conjugal partnership further cements the family's pivotal role in actualizing the common good, a cornerstone of Catholic social doctrine.

As we traverse the Renaissance's intellectual corridors, the ruminations of Desiderius Erasmus emerge with poignant clarity. His emphases on pedagogical reform and moral instruction underscored the centrality of the family in nurturing virtuous citizens. Erasmus critiqued societal and ecclesiastic structures that neglected the familial duty of education, advocating for a home-centric cultivation of piety and wisdom. Through works like "Praise of Folly," Erasmus subtly chastised the vainglorious pursuits that led away from the humble, yet profound mission of familial unity in faith.

The Enlightenment epoch, oft perceived as a crucible of secularism, still saw philosophers whose thoughts interwove with the Catholic paradigm. Blaise Pascal, with his penetrating pensees, delineated the limitations of reason when divorced from divine illumination. His wager, an apologetic reflection on belief, intimates an intrinsic coherence between human finitude and the divine mystery—the family, in his view, becomes a crucible where such existential realities are grappled with and understood. His reflections encourage a contemplative life, where familial bonds are cut from the cloth of spiritual awareness.

Entering the modern era, the existential analyses of Gabriel Marcel offer profound insights into the familial archetype. Marcel's philosophy of the "homo viator"—the man journeying towards fulfillment—resonates with the Catholic nomenclature of the pilgrim church, emphasizing the journey of faith undertaken by each family. He avers that true being is found in relationships, particularly those within the family, which he dubs a "mystery of fidelity" that mirrors divine communion. The ultimate authority, Marcel suggests, is not an oppressive force but an enabling presence that facilitates love and growth within the family structure.

John Paul II, rooted both in theological depth and philosophical acumen, serves as a modern paragon bridging philosophical discourse and papal teaching. His writings, particularly in "Familiaris Consortio" and "Letter to Families," underscore the family as the "first and vital cell of society." His existential personalism highlighted the dignity of each family member, advocating for a reciprocal and participatory relationship that mirrors the divine communion of the Trinity. His pontificate serves as a profound testament to the intertwining of philosophical reflection and steadfast Catholic doctrine, underscoring the essentiality of family in the ecclesiastical mission.

Throughout these epochs, the contributions of philosophers to Catholic thought elucidate the perennial significance of family as it pertains to ecclesial authority and societal ethos. The intricate dance between individual freedom and communal obligation finds its rhythm in the familial structure, sanctified and fostered by the Church's magisterium. Philosophers, from the antediluvian wisdom of Augustine to the contemporary reflections of John Paul II, converge in affirming that the family is both the seedbed of personal virtue and the cornerstone of social harmony.

This intellectual heritage beckons the observer to consider the familial unit not merely as a social institution but as a sanctified entity, ordained and ennobled by divine mandate. In recognizing and venerating the family's role, one discerns the harmonious interplay between philosophical inquiry and theological affirmation, a confluence that strengthens the edifice of Catholic social teaching.

Therefore, in traversing the varied landscapes of philosophic thought, one acknowledges the indelible contributions to Catholic understanding of family and authority. Each philosopher, in their respective era and manner, has bequeathed a legacy that underpins the Church's vision of familial sanctity and communal integrity. Their contemplations echo across the annals of time, inviting the faithful to a deeper, more profound appreciation of the family as the wellspring of moral and spiritual life.

Integrating Sociological and Psychological Insights

As we traverse the philosophic landscape of family and authority within the precious embrace of the Catholic Church, it behooves us to delve into the reservoirs of sociology and psychology. These disciplines, though secular in origin, possess a treasure trove of insights that can augment our understanding of familial structures and the concomitant authority that springs forth from them. Herein lies the convergence of the divine and the learned, where faith embraces reason in a dance as old as time itself.

At the heart of sociological inquiry lies the notion of the family as the foundational unit of society. In the works of Émile Durkheim and Max Weber, one observes an attempt to dissect the myriad ways in which the family shapes and is shaped by societal structures. Durkheim, in particular, posits that the family operates as a microcosm of society, a crucible wherein social norms, values, and roles are first imbibed. For the Catholic, this aligns beautifully with the Church's teaching that the family is the "domestic church," a locus for the initial transmission of faith and morals.

Furthermore, sociology elucidates the intricate web of social relationships that bind us. Through the lens of symbolic interactionism, it is clear that the family is not merely a static institution but a dynamic entity, continually constructed and reconstructed through interactions. These relational tapestries offer Catholics a profound understanding of the familial bonds that are sanctified through the sacraments, particularly marriage. The sacraments, then, are not abstract rituals but deeply relational acts imbued with divine grace, perpetually reaffirming the family's role in God's salvific plan.

Turning to the realm of psychology, we find equally potent insights. Developmental psychology, pioneered by Erik Erikson and furthered by Jean Piaget, reveals the crucial stages of individual growth that occur within the familial context. Erikson's stages of psychosocial development, for instance, underscore the formative role of family in the cultivation of trust, autonomy, and identity. In the nurturing confines of a Catholic family, these stages find their ultimate fulfillment in the embrace of divine Providence, guiding the young soul towards the fullness of life in Christ.

Moreover, attachment theory, a cornerstone of psychological analysis, sheds light on the profound bond between parent and child. John Bowlby's pioneering work in this field reveals that secure attachment fosters a stable and competent adult. For Catholics, this resonates with the divine pedagogy where the parental love mirrors the love of God the Father. Thus, a secure attachment within the family becomes a profound allegory of our attachment to God, rooted in trust and fortified by faith.

In the broader scope of psychological counseling, family systems theory, as advanced by Murray Bowen, offers invaluable insights into the interplay of individual behavior and family dynamics. This systemic view underscores that individual issues often mirror broader familial patterns. Such insights are instrumental for pastoral counseling within the Church, offering a framework to address familial discord while emphasizing the sacramentality of familial bonds. The Church, then, becomes both a sanctuary and a therapeutic community, addressing the holistic needs of its members.

The integration of sociological and psychological scholarship with Catholic doctrine is not without its challenges. One must navigate the delicate balance between embracing useful insights and maintaining doctrinal integrity. Yet, this synthesis is not only possible but necessary. The Catholic intellectual tradition has always been a harmonizing force, reconciling faith with reason, and divine law with human experience. As Thomas Aquinas synthesized Aristotelian philosophy with Christian theology, so too must we weave the empirical insights of modern social sciences into the rich tapestry of Catholic doctrine.

Through discerning integration, we find that sociology and psychology offer fresh perspectives on the exercise of authority within the family. Sociological insights into power dynamics and role expectations can illuminate the Church's teaching on parental authority, which must reflect the loving and sacrificial leadership of Christ. Psychological studies on leadership styles can further elucidate how authority within the family can be both firm and nurturing, mirroring the gentle yet authoritative voice of the Good Shepherd.

In sum, the amalgamation of sociological and psychological insights into the philosophical framework of family and authority enriches our Catholic understanding of these pivotal structures. The family, as conceived within the Catholic tradition, is not merely an isolated unit but a vital cell within the Body of Christ. By drawing upon the empirical wisdom of social sciences, we reaffirm the sacredness of family and the divine ordination of parental authority, all within the grand symphony of God's creation.

Thus, the sacred and the empirical coalesce, offering a profound and holistic vision of family and authority that is both rooted in tradition and responsive to contemporary understandings. As we continue to explore these themes, let us embrace this integrative approach, ever mindful of the divine wisdom that permeates all truth, whether revealed through Scripture, tradition, or the empirical findings of our age.

Chapter 9: Challenges to the Catholic Social Justice Ethos

The Catholic Social Justice Ethos, lofty and noble in its call, encounters myriad tribulations both from without and within. External secular criticisms, oft clad in the guise of progress, cast shadows upon the Church's moral edicts, labeling them as archaic impediments to modern liberty. Meanwhile, house divided cannot stand, and thus internal discord—be it through clerical scandals, doctrinal disagreements, or waning zeal amongst the laity—further shakes the ecclesial edifice. Indeed, the steadfast beacon of Catholic teaching must grapple with the tempestuous sea of contemporary skepticism and dissent. This ongoing crucible tests not merely the resilience of its doctrines but the very sinews of faith and commitment within the community of the faithful, challenging them to reclaim and reaffirm the sanctity of their social mission amidst a world in flux.

Addressing Secular Criticisms

Engaging with the world of secular thought presents a challenge for those who uphold the tenets of Catholic social justice. It casts a critical eye upon our practices, questioning the relevance and applicability of principles rooted in ancient traditions and divine revelation. Such critiques often arise from a misunderstanding or a deliberate dismissal of the spiritual dimensions that infuse our social doctrine. To bring light to these misconceived perspectives, we must delineate the intellectual and moral foundations that render the Catholic vision both timeless and timely.

Primarily, secular criticisms of Catholic social justice hinge upon the perceived anachronism of its teachings. Critics argue that doctrines formulated millennia ago cannot possibly address the nuances and complexities of contemporary society. Yet, it is this very timelessness that imparts resilience and depth to Catholic social teaching. The principles of love, dignity, and justice are not bound by temporal confines; they echo through the annals of history, proving themselves adaptable and enduring. From the writings of St. Augustine to the encyclicals of modern Popes, these principles articulate a vision of humanity that transcends the ephemeral trends and transient ideologies of any given age.

Another point of contention lies in the perceived authoritarianism of the Church's hierarchical structure. Critics, imbued with the spirit of modern individualism, balk at the notion of submitting to an institution that claims divine authority. This critique, however, fails to grasp the ecclesiological truth that the Church, in its authoritative stance, serves as a custodian of divine wisdom—a wisdom meant to guide humanity towards the common good. Far from authoritarian tyranny, the Church's authority is rooted in service, exemplified by Christ washing the feet of his apostles. Herein lies the paradox that secular critics often overlook: true authority in the Church is exercised through humility and self-giving love.

Moreover, secularism often elevates relativism and subjective truth, clashing with the objective moral framework upheld by the Church. In a world that prizes individual autonomy above all else, the immutable moral truths advocated by Catholic social teaching can appear restrictive. Yet, upon closer scrutiny, these truths serve a liberating purpose, safeguarding human dignity and fostering authentic freedom. Moral relativism, by contrast, leads to ethical confusion and societal fragmentation. The Catholic commitment to objective morality provides a sturdy compass in a turbulent sea, offering direction and stability. The Gospel's moral precepts, rather than constraining human potential, foster environments where individuals can thrive within a community oriented toward the common good.

Amidst these larger philosophical objections lies a pragmatic critique: the Church's stance on social issues, particularly those related to life, family, and sexuality. Critics assert that Catholic teachings are out of step with contemporary social values, particularly in areas like LGBTQ+ rights, contraception, and reproductive rights. This criticism cannot be addressed without acknowledging the Church's unwavering commitment to the sanctity of life and the integrity of the family unit. These teachings are not mere doctrinal stances but reflections of a profound reverence for the human person, created in the image and likeness of God. The Church's defense of life from conception to natural death is an affirmation of this sacred dignity, even when it contradicts prevailing social norms.

To respond effectively to such criticisms, Catholics must approach secular interlocutors with both clarity and charity. Engaging in thoughtful dialogue and demonstrating the coherence and compassion of our social teachings can bridge the gap of misunderstanding. This entails not only articulating our principles but also manifesting them through acts of justice and mercy. By living out the tenets of Catholic social teaching in tangible ways, we provide a compelling witness that transcends mere words.

Let us not forget the importance of addressing critiques regarding the Church's historical and contemporary failures. There is no denying that individual members of the Church have, at times, failed to live up to the high standards of our faith. Scandals, abuses, and instances of hypocrisy have sullied our witness and provided ample fodder for secular critics. It is paramount that we approach these issues with honesty, contrition, and a firm resolve to enact reform. The Church's call to justice includes holding itself accountable and striving towards continual purification and renewal.

Furthermore, we must highlight the tremendous good the Church has accomplished and continues to accomplish across the globe. Catholic social teaching, when applied earnestly, has led to the establishment of hospitals, schools, orphanages, and various charitable institutions that serve millions irrespective of their faith. These manifold acts of charity and justice are the fruits of a robust theology that does not disconnect the spiritual from the temporal. The seamless garment of Catholic social teaching weaves together care for the soul with care for the body, showcasing the practical potency of our principles.

When faced with the criticism that the Church is an anachronistic institution, incapable of progressive thought, we must highlight the ongoing development of doctrine and social teaching guided by the Holy Spirit. This dynamic process, while rooted in immutable truths, adapts to new circumstances and challenges without compromising its core values. The social encyclicals of recent Popes, such as Laudato Si' and Fratelli Tutti, reflect a responsive and relevant engagement with contemporary issues like environmental stewardship and global solidarity. These documents affirm the Church's commitment to evolving in response to the signs of the times while remaining steadfast in its fundamental convictions.

In addressing secular criticisms, let us deploy a strategy of informed engagement, rooted in the intellectual tradition of the Church and enriched by pastoral sensitivity. By presenting a cogent defense of our social doctrines, undergirded by reason and revelation, we can confront the challenges posed by secularism not with antagonism but with respectful dialogue. Engagement with secular critiques is not merely a defensive posture but an opportunity for evangelization, inviting others to encounter the transformative power of the Gospel embodied in our social teachings.

In conclusion, the task of addressing secular criticisms of Catholic social justice is multifaceted, requiring both intellectual rigor and pastoral compassion. By articulating the enduring relevance of our teachings, exemplifying their practical application, acknowledging our failures, and celebrating our successes, we bear witness to the profound harmony between faith and reason. In doing so, we invite a world fraught with inconstancy and fragmentation to encounter the enduring truth and transformative love at the heart of the Church's social doctrine.

Responding to Internal Challenges within the Church

Within the sacred enclave of the Church, a myriad of internal challenges arise, seeking to test the fortitude and unity of the Catholic Social Justice ethos. These tribulations do not manifest merely as abstract dilemmas but often precipitate tangible discord and disharmony. In the pursuit of the noble principles of family, community, and participation, the Church must first reckon with its internal intricacies before it can fully project its teachings onto the broader canvas of society.

The perpetual struggle to align the doctrinal purity with the evolving societal demands presents a formidable challenge. The Church, steeped in tradition, is oftentimes viewed as immutable, even anachronistic, by its detractors within. Efforts to modernize or adapt are not always universally welcomed, eliciting resistance rooted in a deep reverence for historical continuity. Hence, an equilibrium must be cultivated — one that honors tradition while embracing necessary change, lest the institution becomes ossified and disconnected from its flock.

Clerical celibacy, for instance, has long been a cornerstone of the Church's spiritual discipline. However, this practice has sparked considerable debate even within the hallowed echelons. Some argue that celibacy is indispensable, signifying a total devotion to God, untethered by earthly bonds. Others contend that re-evaluating this discipline could alleviate numerous pastoral challenges and better reflect the communal and familial essence of Catholic teachings. The resolution lies not in outright abolishment or stringent defense but in a compassionate, deliberate discourse informed by theological, spiritual, and practical insights.

Moreover, the role of the laity in ecclesiastical governance continues to be a crucible of much contention. A progressive inclusion of laypersons in various ministerial roles is perceived by some as essential to the vitality and relevance of the Church. Nonetheless, this transitional approach must not undermine the authority vested in the ordained clergy. Striking a harmonious balance where both clergy and laity function synergistically is paramount. Herein lies a microcosm of Catholic social justice — fostering a spirit of cooperation and mutual respect.

Notably, financial transparency within the Church's administrative mechanisms poses another significant internal challenge. The pursuit of social justice predicates upon the moral imperative of honesty and integrity. Instances of financial mismanagement or opacity not only tarnish the Church's image but also erode the trust of its faithful. Instituting rigorous oversight, embracing transparency, and fostering a culture of accountability are critical steps in safeguarding the moral and ethical foundation upon which the Church stands.

A particular thorn in the Church's side is the handling of clerical abuse cases. This grave issue has caused immeasurable pain and has significantly undermined trust. The Church's response must be unequivocal and resolute — prioritizing the welfare and dignity of victims, ensuring justice is served, and implementing preventive measures to safeguard the sanctity of all its members, particularly the vulnerable. This issue transcends mere policy; it is a profound moral reckoning, calling for sincere repentance and committed reform.

Doctrinal disagreements also underscore the internal dynamics of the Church. Contemporary issues such as the stance on LGBTQ+ matters, divorce, and remarriage have engendered significant debate. Enriching this discourse with empathy and open-mindedness while upholding core tenets of faith is vital. In navigating these contentious waters, the Church must exemplify its foundational imperatives of love, mercy, and justice.

Furthermore, generational gaps and varying levels of theological understanding among the faithful can lead to fragmentation. The digital age presents both a challenge and an opportunity in this regard. Effective catechesis tailored to varying demographics and leveraging modern communication channels can bridge these divides, fostering a united, well-informed community poised to embody and propagate the Church's social teachings.

Another internal challenge rests in maintaining the integrity of liturgy and worship. Liturgical practices, rich in symbolism and tradition, are the heartbeat of Catholic worship. However, the call for liturgical reform resonates within certain quarters, driven by a desire for more engaging and inclusive worship experiences. The Church must navigate these desiderata judiciously, preserving the sanctity and profundity of the liturgy while ensuring it remains a living, vibrant expression of faith.

The clerical hierarchy's rigidity is often criticized as another impediment to the Church's harmonious function. In addressing this, an inclusive approach to leadership that embraces dialogue and collective wisdom should be cultivated. This progression must not signify a departure from doctrinal fidelity but rather an enlightened understanding of governance that mirrors the just and participatory society the Church advocates for.

Finally, the enduring challenge of fostering a true sense of community within the Church cannot be understated. The faithful, often dispersed and diverse, must feel a genuine sense of belonging and participation. Initiatives that promote active engagement, communal support, and inclusiveness are essential. Within this framework, the Church exemplifies the very principles it seeks to instill in society at large.

In conclusion, addressing these internal challenges with wisdom, compassion, and a steadfast commitment to core Catholic values will fortify the Church's social justice mission. It will enable the Church not merely to weather the storms within but to emerge more united and resilient, reflecting a vibrant testament to faith, family, community, and participation.

Chapter 10: Strategies for Promoting Catholic Social Justice

To advance the cause of Catholic social justice, one must wield a multilayered approach that marries time-honored tradition with the exigencies of modernity. This endeavor requires a seamless fusion of effective apologetics with sustained initiatives aimed at bolstering family and community life. It is through these unions that the sacred value of human dignity finds its deepest resonance, fortifying the public and private domains where faith seeks manifestation. Enkindling the spirit of solidarity, fostering active participation within ecclesiastical and civic spheres, and vigorously defending the moral imperatives of the Church become our clarion call. Moreover, this pursuit implores us to engage with and adapt to contemporary societal pressures without diluting the immutable truths that form the bedrock of our beliefs. By employing advocacy, education, and community outreach, we create a dynamic mosaic where faith and reason, tradition and innovation, converge to elevate the human condition in the light of divine wisdom.

Methods for Effective Apologetics

In the realm of Catholic social justice, effective apologetics serve as the crucible for refining and defending the moral and theological tenets of our faith. The Apostolic virtue of apologetics is neither merely an exercise in sophistic erudition nor a rhetorical flourish; it is the lifeblood of doctrinal vitality and communal integrity. Through methods steeped in tradition yet alive with contemporary relevance, we may engage both heart and mind to advocate for the profound call to family, community, and participation.

Let us dwell first on the necessity of understanding our audience, for apologetics unfurled without cognizance of the listener's context frequently descends into futility. The astute apologist considers the existential and cultural preconditions that perplex the modern mind. This understanding should not be superficial but must delve into sociological insights and psychological textures, which frequently dictate how the tenets of the Church might be received or resisted. Thus, one's defense of the family, the sanctity of community, and the essential call to participation must be empathic yet unwavering.

Beyond understanding, there lies the essentiality of coherence. To articulate the veracity of Catholic social justice, the apologist's discourse ought to be integrative—knitting seamlessly the Holy Scriptures, the magisterial teachings, and the lived experience of faith. This triadic foundation lends invincibility to our argumentation. The coherence inherently springs from unity in diversity within the myriad expressions of Catholic doctrine, manifesting divine wisdom through multiple yet harmonious voices.

Moreover, the apologist should wield the power of narrative as a potent method. Parables once gleaned wisdom from common life, and so too can our apologetics in advocacy for social justice. Stories of families transformed through faith, communities uplifted by communal participation, and individual lives turned toward the divine light offer living testaments that abstract syllogisms cannot match. Narratives bridge the chasm between heady doctrine and palpable reality.

In the practice of rhetoric, the classical art of persuasion must be revitalized. Employing the Aristotelian ethos, pathos, and logos remains forever pertinent. Ethos—embodying moral character—inspires trust. Pathos—stirring the appropriate emotional response—awakens zeal. Logos—logical consistency and clarity—satisfies the intellect. Such eloquence, balanced and holistic, is indispensable in defending Catholic social teaching amidst a skeptical or indifferent world.

Let us not neglect the apologetic method of dialogical engagement. St. Paul, that eagle of the divine dialectic, demonstrates the unmatched value of dialogue in his Pauline letters and public discourses. He engages, questions, listens, and then responds, always grounding his discourse on divinely revealed truth. Thus, modern apologetics must similarly cherish dialogue over monologue, fostering a contaminatio—a mingling of perspectives that enriches both interlocutor and listener.

Equipping oneself with a scholarly arsenal is yet another vital method. Mastery of seminal Church documents, such as "Pacem in Terris" and "Gaudium et Spes," provides the apologist with the jurisprudence of Catholic thought. A familiarity with key encyclicals and catechisms affords one the doctrinal precision necessary for persuasive argumentation. Furthermore, a dialogic engagement with contemporary sociological and psychological studies shall offer empirical robustness to theological assertions.

Analogous to this, we venture into the importance of humility in our apologetic endeavors. The haughty disposition renders even the most cogent arguments odious. Christ Himself, embodying divine humility, attracts through self-emptying love. So too must the apologist approach every conversation as a servant, seeking not to conquer but to enlighten and edify. Humility catalyzes a receptive atmosphere where truth can be perceived, embraced, and loved.

Assign then, a role to the sacramental life. The living out of the sacraments transforms apologetics from theoretical postulation into existential reality. The Eucharist, Confirmation, and Reconciliation become sacraments of sustained argument: living proofs of our doctrines through embodied practice. Through them, the truths we defend find vivid exemplification and the hearts of skeptics may be similarly incarnated in grace.

Furthermore, an apologist must interweave prayer into his or her methods. Intercessory prayers allied with personal piety infuse apologetic efforts with divine favor. Prayer is not merely a preamble but an ongoing accompaniment, a scaffold upon which our testimonies and defenses stand firm. St. Augustine well knew the efficacy of prayer when he exclaimed, "Our hearts are restless until they rest in Thee."

Lastly, embracing the comprehensive catholicity—the "according to the whole" nature of the Church—is crucial. Our apologetics must echo St. Cyprian's axiom, "No one can have God as Father who does not have the Church as Mother." This ecclesial unity strengthens our apologia as it nests within the praxis of an ongoing, lived tradition. The vibrant testimonies of the saints, the communal liturgies, and the steadfast institution itself serve as bulwarks for our social doctrines.

Thus, dear adherents of a faith that refuses compartmentalization but seeks holistic integration, may these methods serve to not only defend but also vivify our sublime call to social justice as articulated by the perennial wisdom of Holy Mother Church. Through judicious application and ceaseless prayer, may our apologetics be both a beacon of truth and an embrace of divine love.

Initiatives for Family and Community Enhancement

In the realms of Catholic Social Justice, the family stands as the cornerstone upon which the edifice of community is constructed. The initiatives for enhancing this pivotal unit transcend mere programmatic efforts; they are, indeed, a spiritual and moral mandate. The Church, imbued with her sacrosanct mission, must craft initiatives that not only sustain but elevate the family to its divine vocation.

Foremost among these initiatives is the fostering of environments that are conducive to the spiritual growth and moral development of families. A community cannot flourish without strong familial bonds, and as such, it is imperative to create spaces where families feel supported and nurtured. Parishes must become sanctuaries of solace and platforms for open dialogue, where families can engage in both spiritual and social activities, thereby fortifying their collective identity.

Benevolent actions rooted in Catholic teaching must manifest through both ecclesiastical guidance and lay participation. The compounding power of collective efforts reveals itself in initiatives that are co-created by clergy and laity. Such collaborations can take the form of family retreats, workshops, and counseling sessions—each designed to address the myriad facets of familial life from spiritual nourishment to practical welfare.

Moreover, the Church must emphasize catechesis tailored specifically for families. Educational programs should not merely reiterate doctrinal truths but facilitate a deeper understanding of how these truths can be lived out within the family context. This calls for a blend of theological instruction and real-life applications, thus allowing the sacred teachings to permeate daily existence.

In addition to spiritual endeavors, the Church should advocate for social policies that protect and empower families. This includes taking active stances on issues such as affordable housing, healthcare, and education. By championing these causes, the Church embodies the principles of social justice, extending her mission beyond the walls of the sanctuary and into the broader societal fabric.

Communal support systems are equally quintessential. Initiatives such as family support groups within the parish can serve as lifelines for those experiencing trials and tribulations. In these groups, members can share experiences, offer advice, and extend spiritual and emotional support, thereby building a tighter-knit community.

Activities that involve the whole community, such as parish-wide celebrations, can foster unity and a sense of belonging. These events should exemplify the family's role as the nucleus of communal life, encouraging participation from all members—from the youngest to the eldest. By doing so, the Church reinforces the familial bonds that are the underpinning of social harmony.

A unique and profound initiative could be the establishment of mentorship programs, wherein seasoned families guide and support younger or struggling families. These connections, rooted in Christian love and understanding, can provide invaluable counsel and reassurance, showcasing the transformational power of collective wisdom and shared experiences.

Further, the Church must not neglect the role of technology in modern family life. Initiatives should include resources and guidance on prudent and ethical use of digital technology, helping families to navigate the challenges and opportunities presented by the digital age. This might encompass workshops on digital literacy, online safety, and ethical considerations in the consumption of media.

In the liturgical aspect, every effort should be made to integrate families into the sacred mysteries celebrated by the Church. This can be achieved through family-centered liturgies and involving family units in various liturgical roles. Such participations allow families to experience the unity and sanctity that underpin the Christian faith, further anchoring them in the divine mission.

Pastoral care, particularly sensitive to the unique challenges faced by families, must be a priority. This includes providing resources for issues such as marital strife, parental guidance, and youth mentorship. Guided by the compassionate heart of Christ, the Church must extend her pastoral care to every family, leaving none to fend alone in their struggles.

One must also consider the intergenerational aspect of family life. Initiatives that promote interactions between different age groups within the family and the broader community can foster mutual respect and understanding. Elder members can impart wisdom and heritage, while the younger generation brings vibrancy and fresh perspectives, resulting in a harmonious and cohesive community.

The Church must also inspire families to enact social change. Encouraging family participation in social justice causes, such as food drives, community clean-ups, and visits to the elderly, can instill values of service and altruism. These actions, grounded in the Gospel, allow families to witness firsthand the transformative power of love in action.

In summary, initiatives for family and community enhancement must be multifaceted, addressing spiritual, social, and practical needs. They should resonate with the holistic vision of Catholic Social Justice, wherein the family, nurtured in faith and action, becomes the bedrock of a just and compassionate society. By lifting up families, the Church not only fulfills her sacred mission but also constructs a community that mirrors the Kingdom of God.

Embrace these initiatives with the wisdom that the bedrock of society is indeed the family. Within the sanctum of the family lies the potential to transform communities, reaffirming the magnificence of souls committed to the collective good. As such, these initiatives serve not merely as tasks but as a divine vocation—guiding families toward their highest calling in the tapestry of God's grand design.

Chapter 11: The Role of Education in Social Justice and Apologetics

In the grand tapestry of Catholicism, education doth play a most pivotal role in weaving the principles of social justice and the art of apologetics into the very fabric of our communal consciousness. By enlightening the minds and souls of the faithful through catechesis, the Church doth empower individuals and families to act justly and defend the faith with a fervor both reasoned and compassionate. In this wise, education becometh not merely an academic endeavor, but a sacred duty that unites philosophical rigor with the moral imperatives of our tradition. Through diligent instruction in both ecclesiastical and societal tenets, we equip the laity to navigate the complexities of modernity while steadfastly upholding the timeless truths of the Gospel. Thus, the mantle of education carrieth the weight of our forebears' wisdom, extending the reach of divine justice and the sanctity of ecclesial authority to every corner of the human experience.

Catechesis and Social Teaching

The intertwining of catechesis and social teaching weaves a tapestry both divine and temporal, enshrining the values of Catholic pedagogy within the framework of greater societal quest. From apostolic times, the Church has endeavored to illuminate truth, fostering souls towards the eternal Kingdom whilst addressing the vicissitudes of earthly existence. This dual mission captivates the essence of education in our quest for social justice and the fervent apologetics that defend the sanctity of the Church's teachings.

In the hallowed halls of catechesis, one discovers a profound commitment to instilling the principles underpinning Catholic social teaching. These principles aren't mere philosophical abstractions; they are the real, tangible expressions of divine love and justice manifest in our daily lives. The Lord's mandate, "Love thy neighbor as thyself," reverberates through the annals of time, challenging us to create a just society aligned with divine will.

Central to this undertaking is the principle of human dignity, an irrefutable cornerstone upon which all social teachings rest. The Church instructs that every human life is sacred, bearing the imprint of the Creator. In catechetical instruction, educators underscore the inviolability of human dignity, which stands as a bulwark against injustice. This commitment extends to all facets of life, from the unborn to the marginalized, ensuring that all are enveloped in the grace of our Maker.

Another pillar upon which Catholic social teaching stands is the preferential option for the poor and vulnerable. Through catechesis, the faithful are nurtured to recognize and respond to the cries of the impoverished, emulating Christ's own ministry among the desolate and outcast. This theological tenet calls for a personal and communal conversion, steering our focus towards the needs of our less fortunate brethren and demanding that structures of society be reoriented in favor of justice and mercy.

The principle of solidarity serves as an adhesive, binding personal piety to communal well-being. Within the catechetical sphere, educators emphasize that we are all part of one human family. It is an invitation to transcend parochial allegiances and embrace a universal kinship rooted in divine love. Solidarity implores us to stand with our brothers and sisters in their struggles, fostering a spirit of unity and support that transcends borders.

Yet, solidarity finds its complement in the principle of subsidiarity. The Church, through catechesis, teaches that higher authorities must respect and support the initiative of smaller communities without usurping their roles. It is an advocacy for local action and individual empowerment—a notion that true justice is most effectively realized when communities are entrusted with their own fate, supported rather than supplanted by larger institutions.

Indeed, the Church's social doctrine, as imparted through catechesis, seeks to balance these principles within the context of an individual's integral human development. Pope Paul VI's exhortation in "Populorum Progressio," is a seminal text examining the notion that authentic development must promote the flourishing of every human capability and vocation. Catechesis thus becomes a vehicle for imbuing the faithful with an understanding that true progress is defined not by material accumulation but by the holistic growth of every person's physical, spiritual, and moral dimensions.

This holistic vision is further enshrined in the principle of the common good. Within catechesis, the faithful are called to orient their actions towards the common good, fostering environments where communal peace and prosperity are attainable. The common good is not a mere aggregation of individual goods; rather, it is the overall conditions necessary for people to flourish together. This extends to ensuring rights are upheld, safeguarding social conditions that allow for the full participation of all members in the life of society.

Moreover, the Church's social instruction underscores the importance of promoting peace and justice. Catechesis reminds the faithful that peace is not merely the absence of war but the presence of conditions conducive to justice. St. Augustine's profound insight that "peace is the tranquility of order," is intricately explored in catechetical sessions, encouraging those taught to become peacemakers in their own right, addressing discord through a framework of justice tempered with mercy.

The educational mission of the Church is incomplete without the contextualization of these social doctrines within a scriptural and theological paradigm. Scriptural exegesis in catechesis provides the bedrock for understanding these principles not as contemporary innovations but as truths deeply rooted in sacred tradition. Scriptural models, like the Good Samaritan, serve as pedagogical tools, retelling essential lessons that underscore compassionate engagement and charitable action.

A salient feature of catechesis is its commitment to the integration of social teaching amidst diverse cultural and temporal contexts. It demands that social principles be neither static nor monolithic but dynamic, engaging with the contours of different societal frameworks while remaining anchored to immutable truths. Catechesis, therefore, becomes a bridge spanning the eternal truths of the Gospel and the temporal challenges of contemporary society.

The role of catechetical education in this endeavor is further enriched through its symbiotic relationship with other academic disciplines. Philosophers and sociologists provide critical lenses through which the tenets of social teaching can be scrutinized and contextualized, while psychologists offer insights into the human condition that enhance pastoral care and social engagement. This interdisciplinary approach, cultivated within catechetical instruction, fashions a more robust and empathetic understanding of social justice.

In conclusion, catechesis is not merely a transmission of doctrine but a transformative process challenging the faithful to embody social justice in their lives. It is the linchpin connecting individual faith to broader societal obligation, ensuring that theological principles are incarnated within the structures of human interaction. The synergy between catechesis and social teaching is essential to realizing the Church's mission, fostering a world where divine love and justice are concretely practiced, bringing forth the Kingdom of God in our midst.

Educating Families and Parishes

In the celestial sphere of human society, the salient role of education cannot be overstated. The edifice of education serves as the linchpin of social justice, and more pointedly, in the realm of Catholic apologetics. The dissemination of knowledge, particularly concerning the intricate tenets of Catholic doctrine, must first anchor itself within the sanctified environments of family and parish.

The family, often extolled as the domestic church, is where the ennoblement of spirit and intellect should commence. Here, in the sanctity of familial bonds, the first whispers of divine instruction imbue young minds with virtuous inclinations, sowing the seeds for a life led in justice and truth. The tender years of youth, while malleable, are fertile ground. It is within this cradle of nascent morality and intellectual pursuit that education must be deeply imbued with the principles of Catholic social teaching.

In parishes, this sacred task continues under the auspices of ordained ministers, catechists, and the community. The embodied Word made flesh, manifest in the Sacraments, becomes the wellspring from which divine knowledge flows. Each sanctuary is not merely a venue for the celebration of the liturgical calendar but is equally a haven for lifelong learning. Yet, there must be a synthesis, wherein the sacred domicile and the hallowed ecclesiastical space work in harmonious tandem.

For education in families and parishes to be efficacious, it must transcend rote memorization of doctrine. It should instead cultivate a profound understanding and a heartfelt zeal for the Church's social mission. Pedagogy must be suffused with the warmth of love and the ardor of conviction, ensuring that the ethos of social justice is not just taught but caught through example and lived experience. Such harmonic instruction serves as both the sword and shield in the apologetical defense of the faith.

Consider the impact of catechesis that focuses on integrating Scripture with the exigencies of contemporary life. If families and parishes delve into the Gospels, extracting practical lessons on mercy, justice, and communal harmony, they create a nexus where faith and reason meet. Let not the sacred texts remain arcane inscriptions but living words that enkindle social action and foster an unwavering commitment to the common good.

Noteworthy too, is the strategic importance of educating adult members within the family and parish. While much emphasis is placed upon the formative years of youth, the continuing education of adults cannot languish. The maturity of thought and the depth of wisdom that adults possess provide fertile terrain for sophisticated theological reflections and robust social action. Parishes ought to conduct regular discussions, workshops, and study groups that focus on critical issues, affirming the relevance of Church teachings in addressing modern social maladies.

Moreover, the symbiotic relationship between families and parishes thrives on communal learning experiences. Pilgrimages, retreats, and service projects where families partake in concert with their parish community can be potent means of education. These immersive experiences extend beyond the didactic and enter the realm of kinesthetic learning, where faith and works unite. When families labor side by side in social justice initiatives, they not only self-purify but also provide a luminous testament to the world of what it means to live out the Gospel.

The methodology employed in educating families and parishes also bears careful scrutiny. It must be dialogical rather than monological, inviting participation rather than passive reception. Therein lies the essence of true education—an active engagement with content and context, fostering critical thinking, and encouraging questions. Parishes should serve as forums where the laity feels empowered to voice their experiences and insights, thus enriching the communal understanding of social justice and apologetics.

In the rich mosaic of Catholic education, technology's judicious use presents both opportunities and challenges. Digital catechesis, online study tools, and virtual fellowship can supplement traditional forms of learning. Yet, one must be wary of technology's propensity to atomize and isolate rather than unite. Therefore, any technological integration should be scrutinized to ensure it enhances rather than detracts from communal identity and spiritual solidarity.

Furthermore, ecclesiastical hierarchy and clergy must be unwavering in their commitment to fostering educational programs that uphold the Church's social doctrines. Bishop shepherds and parish priests are called to be exemplars, mentors, and teachers in the vineyard of Christ. They must ensure that educational initiatives sponsored within their parishes remain doctrinally sound and socially responsive.

Indeed, education in social justice and apologetics within families and parishes cannot be construed merely as an ancillary duty. It is integral, for in the proper instruction of the faithful lies the preservation of faith itself. To educate is to equip for both defense and discipleship, arming the intellect and the spirit against the turmoils of the temporal world. To neglect this is to render the faithful vulnerable to the philosophical sophistries and moral relativism so prevalent in secular discourse.

In sum, the paramount task of educating families and parishes is one to be approached with gravity, fervor, and profound dedication. It is not a static endeavor but a dynamic journey, one that continually calls for renewal, reflection, and recommitment. Through such diligent efforts, the holy institutions of family and parish may flourish, radiating the luminous truths of Catholic social justice and fortifying the community in the irrefutable wisdom of apologetics.

Thus, let the clarion call resound within every Catholic home and parish, echoing the eternal verities engraved by Divine Providence upon the human heart. In this noble pursuit, families and parishes shall emerge as beacons of light in a world oft enveloped in darkness, steadfast custodians of the faith, and diligent stewards of the Church's timeless mission of justice and truth.

Chapter 12: Future Directions for Catholic Social Justice and Apologetics

Gazing into the firmament of tomorrow, one discerns both trials and triumphs that shall shape the future of Catholic Social Justice and Apologetics. Herein lies a call to prophesy; a clarion beckoning the faithful to envision a horizon where the sanctity of family, the vitality of community, and the spirit of participation conjoin in a symphony of divine love and human endeavor. Emerging trends and dilemmas cast shadows and light upon this path, yet it is through grappling with such dualities that faith is both tested and fortified. Let the progeny of our ecclesiastical and philosophical undertaking be guided by a vision that marries doctrinal rigor with the exigencies of contemporary exigency. Thus, let the beatific hope be our torchbearer, as we, in the spirit of communion, forge a future where justice and apologetics are not disparate entities but harmonious notes in the great canticle of creation.

Emerging Trends and Issues

As the dawn of a new era approaches, the symbiotic relationship between Catholic social justice and apologetics undergoes a metamorphosis, influenced by multifarious currents of contemporary thought and socio-cultural upheavals. One discerns an inexorable shift towards inter-religious dialogue, wherein the Catholic Church, cognizant of its universal mission, embraces ecumenism in unprecedented ways. The magisterial dialogues seek not merely mutual respect but a convergence of efforts towards universal justice and peace.

Paramount amongst these trends is the burgeoning role of laity in social justice initiatives, transcending traditional ecclesiastical boundaries. No longer are matters of doctrine and practice sequestered in the cloisters of the ordained; rather, a clarion call reverberates through the pews, urging lay Catholics to embody the Church's social teachings in the public square. From grassroots movements advocating for the sanctity of life to social enterprises addressing economic disparities, the laity's participation redefines the ethos of ecclesial engagement.

Furthermore, digital technology infuses the realm of Catholic apologetics with new vigor and reach. The proliferation of online platforms, social media, and digital evangelization projects invigorates apologetic discourse, targeting not just the faithful but also the skeptics and the seekers. These technological advancements serve not only as vehicles for dissemination but also as arenas for vibrant, instantaneous, and interactive theological discussions.

The Church confronts ethical quandaries emerging from advancements in biotechnology and artificial intelligence. Questions about the sanctity of life, human dignity, and the moral implications of genetic manipulation pose profound challenges, demanding a rearticulation of foundational principles in light of scientific progress. In response, Catholic ethicists and theologians labor assiduously to provide guidance, ensuring that technological advancements do not undermine the immutable tenets of human worth and divine providence.

The burgeoning environmental crisis also commands the Church's attentive discernment. Embodying the principles articulated in Pope Francis's encyclical "Laudato Si'," there is a palpable shift towards environmental stewardship as a manifestation of social justice. Catholic communities worldwide undertake initiatives to foster sustainable practices, reinforcing the concept that care for creation is inextricably linked to care for humanity.

One cannot overlook the profound impact of migration and globalization on the paradigms of community and participation. The ever-increasing movement of peoples across borders necessitates a re-evaluation of the Church's role in fostering inclusive, multi-ethnic communities. The principles of universal fraternity and solidarity are put to the test as the Church strives to be a beacon of hope and a home for diverse populations, addressing both their spiritual and temporal needs.

Additionally, the Church faces the delicate task of reconciling tradition with modernity, particularly in the realm of gender roles and family structures. While upholding the sanctity and primacy of the traditional family unit, the Church must also navigate the complexities introduced by evolving societal norms and legal frameworks surrounding marriage, parenting, and gender identity. This necessitates a delicate balance, affirming doctrinal truths while extending pastoral care and compassion.

The intersection of mental health and spiritual well-being emerges as a critical area of focus. The modern scourge of anxiety, depression, and existential despair calls for an integrative approach wherein psychological insights are harmonized with spiritual guidance. Catholic pastoral care is increasingly incorporating therapeutic practices, underscoring the Church's commitment to holistic well-being.

Moreover, the Church's social justice efforts are increasingly scrutinized within the broader context of global geopolitics. As nations grapple with conflicts and power dynamics, the Church's voice in advocating for peace, justice, and the dignity of the human person assumes a prophetic dimension. The influence of Catholic social teachings on international policies and humanitarian efforts testifies to the Church's enduring relevance in the global arena.

An emergent trend involves the Church's engagement with youth and millennial Catholics, whose experiences and perceptions are molded by an era of unprecedented information access and socio-political activism. To resonate with this demographic, the Church must adopt innovative catechetical methods and foster environments where young Catholics can actively engage in social justice initiatives, thus ensuring that the torch of faith and justice passes unquenched to future generations.

The rise of secularism and relativism presents formidable challenges to the authority of the Catholic Church. In a milieu where absolute truths are often eschewed, Catholic apologetics finds itself defending the objective reality of Church teachings against the tide of subjective moral frameworks. Articulating a coherent and compelling defense of faith necessitates a renewed emphasis on reason, natural law, and the enduring wisdom embedded in Catholic tradition.

In conclusion, the Church stands at the nexus of myriad currents shaping the future of social justice and apologetics. The call to family, community, and participation remains unwavering, yet the pathways to realizing these ideals are continuously redefined by emerging trends and issues. As the Church navigates these uncharted waters, its enduring mission remains clear: to bear witness to the truth, uphold the dignity of the human person, and manifest the love of Christ in an ever-changing world.

Long-term Vision for Family, Community, and Participation

In the grand tapestry of Catholic social justice, the interwoven threads of family, community, and participation create an intricate pattern that reveals the divine plan for humanity. The long-term vision we must hold embraces an ever-deeper commitment to these foundational elements, for they are not merely constructs of social order but are deeply rooted in the theological and philosophical bedrock of our faith.

The family, often heralded as the "domestic church," serves as the nucleus of society. This sacred institution extends beyond biological kinship to encompass spiritual kinship, reflecting the Trinitarian relationship of Father, Son, and Holy Spirit. Our vision for the future must, therefore, prioritize policies and practices that fortify family bonds, ensuring that they become resilient bastions of faith, hope, and love in an increasingly fragmented world.

Through a lens sharpened by ecclesiastical and scriptural insights, one perceives that the family is not an entity to be considered in isolation. Rather, it flourishes within the greater vine of community. Just as a vine supports and nourishes its branches, so does the broader community sustain the family unit, offering a network of spiritual, social, and economic interdependence. In our pursuit of a long-horizon view, fostering such interconnectedness must be integral.

Beneath the shelter of this overarching canopy of community, individual dignity and the common good find their harmonious balance. The Church has always implored its faithful to actively participate in the life of the community, seeing each person's involvement as a vital contribution to the moral and civic health of society. Therefore, in gazing into the future, the imperative rests on nurturing environments where each member can participate fully, honoring their God-given talents and callings.

Long-term vision necessitates an unwavering gaze on educational endeavors that inculcate the principles of Catholic social justice within our youth. Through catechesis and beyond, we must imbue future generations with an understanding that family life and community engagement are not merely optional pathways but the divine will's primary avenues. This includes emphasizing the symbiotic relationship between the Church's teachings and the psychological and sociological well-being of individuals.

To ensure our vision does not become a mere idealistic mirage, practical measures will be essential. Herein lies the importance of fostering grassroots structures that allow laypeople to exercise their co-responsibility in ecclesial life and civic spaces. Whether it's through parish councils, local social initiatives, or educational outreach programs, the seeds sown today will yield abundant harvests in the future.

Moreover, in casting our eyes forward, we must heed the historical lessons embedded within the Church's encounters with modernity's challenges. The reciprocity between authority and laity, between papal guidance and family fidelity, must anchor our vision. This dynamic interplay will serve as both the compass and the anchor amidst the vicissitudes of time and culture.

As the relentless march of time progresses, so too must our dialogue with the secular world. Our vision entails not only shielding ourselves within the comfort of tradition but also engaging with contemporary social issues through the expansive lens of Catholic social doctrine. Envisioning robust frameworks where families can thrive—despite the myriad economic, environmental, and social challenges—requires looking beyond merely ecclesial borders and building alliances that advance the common good.

Here lies the call for prophetic witness—living examples of families and communities that bear testament to the transformative power of the Gospel. It is through these living icons that the broader world can witness the efficacy of Catholic social principles. Thus, nurturing such witnesses becomes a key imperative in our long-term pastoral strategies.

In conclusion, our long-term vision for family, community, and participation revolves around a tripartite axis of theological fidelity, social engagement, and educational endeavors. Each segment of this triad must be vigorously pursued and harmonized, such that the resultant symphony resounds through the corridors of time, an enduring testament to the divine wisdom embodied within our Catholic faith. Through concerted effort, guided by grace, we tread this path, ever aspiring to embody the kingdom of God within our earthly sojourn.

Conclusion

The corridors of time echo with the unchanging resonance of the Catholic Church's call to family, community, and active participation. As we approach the denouement of this treatise, we must survey the mosaic we have crafted, mindful of the intricacies that bind the practical to the divine, the human to the ecclesiastical, and the temporal to the eternal. Indeed, it is in the nexus of these realms that one finds the soul of Catholic Social Justice.

Behold, the family stands as the primordial cell of society. From the Genesis of mankind, family has functioned as the first echo of the divine symphony, implying that every familial bond is laced with sacred threads. The Scriptures illuminate this truth with the soft yet unwavering glow of eternal wisdom. Thus, in nourishing and protecting the sanctity of family, we uphold the very essence of divine communality. Every moment spent in support of familial bonds contributes to the rejuvenation of the societal organism.

Moreover, the family's role is not merely a passive existence but an active cornerstone upon which communities are constructed. The family becomes the crucible of social virtue, fostering within its humble confines the citizens of tomorrow. As the Catholic Church has consistently taught, the family prepares one to engage in both the civic and ecclesiastical domains with a heart poised to serve and hands ready to labor. The seedbed of virtue in the family germinates into the tree of social participation, yielding fruits of both spiritual and communal bounty.

It is here, in the interaction between family, community, and the broader society, that the Church extends her maternal arms, guiding her children with the twin lanterns of doctrine and tradition. The authority of the Catholic Church, irrefutably supported through historical continuity and theological profundity, serves as the scaffolding for our engagement in the communal and societal spheres. The Church, as both teacher and mother, whispers her guidance through the ages, enabling the faithful to navigate the moral conundrums of contemporary existence.

At the same time, the lively participation of the laity in both Church and civic life breathes vigor into the corpus of Catholic Social Justice. Through active participation, the faithful discern their vocation not as isolated beings but as integral parts of a larger divine plan. Their efforts in the communal halls of parishes, the bustling agora of public discourse, and the quiet sanctuaries of family life serve as tangible manifestations of an internalized faith. By such means, the Church's social doctrines are not mere abstract principles but lived realities.

In our exploration of balance, we have traversed the intersection of theological dogma and social imperatives, harmonizing the sacred with the practical. This harmonization is a testament to the adaptability and eternal relevance of Catholic teachings. It underscores that while the world may wax and wane in its ideologies, the truths imparted by the Church remain inviolable. To engage in Catholic Social Justice is thus to participate in a movement of eternal significance, one that transcends the ephemeral debates of the secular world.

We also reviewed the venerated and modern-day exemplars of this social action, recognizing that Catholic Social Justice is not confined to theoretical musings. It is a mission propelled by both historical precedents and contemporary necessity. The canon of saints and the ordinary faithful alike demonstrate that unwavering commitment to the principles of Catholic teaching brings about tangible change in the world.

The philosophies and sciences of the human condition have further augmented our understanding, providing nuanced perspectives that enrich Catholic thought. The engagement of sociological and psychological insights allows us to address human suffering and societal malaise not through cold analysis but with compassionate rationale, rooted firmly in the love of Christ. These disciplines, when faithfully integrated into the Church's mission, ensure a holistic approach to building communities and supporting families.

Yet, amidst these affirmations, we are not blind to the challenges that loom. Both external critiques and internal tribulations seek to undermine the very edifice of Catholic Social Justice. The secular world, with its transient enthusiasms and fleeting convictions, often stands in opposition. Within the Church, crises of faith and comprehension demand an ever-vigilant and robust apologetic response. Herein lies the urgency of fostering resilient strategies that align orthodox beliefs with dynamic, empathetic approaches to contemporary issues.

In doing so, the role of education emerges as a pillar that cannot be overstated. Catechesis and comprehensive social teachings fortify the faithful, equipping them to confront both ideological adversaries and societal injustices with unyielding conviction and informed compassion. The torchbearers of tomorrow's Church must be adequately prepared to advocate for family, community, and active participation in a world that sorely needs these virtuous constructs.

As we look toward the horizon of future direction, we envisage a Church that continues to anticipate and address emerging trends and issues. With eyes unclouded by temporal allurements, the long-term vision of the Church focuses on fostering environments where families thrive, communities flourish, and every individual understands their irreplaceable role in the divine tapestry. It is a vision anchored in the timeless truths of the faith, imbued with hope and an unwavering commitment to justice.

In the final analysis, the journey through the prisms of Catholic Social Justice illuminated the indivisibility of faith and action. The call to family, community, and participation is not merely an echo of ancient teachings but a present imperative. The Church, vested with divine authority and eternal wisdom, remains the guiding star through the turbulence of modernity, beckoning all to a higher, united purpose.

Thus, let this conclusion serve not as an end but as an impetus—a clarion call to carry forth the principles of Catholic Social Justice into every sphere of life. Let us, as faithful stewards, continue to build and nourish the foundational pillars of family, community, and participation, confident in the knowledge that in doing so, we partake in a sacred mission that transcends the ages.

Appendix A: Appendix

Within this appendix, thou shalt discover a treasure trove of sacred parchments and pivotal texts that undergird the noble edifice of Catholic Social Justice, particularly as it pertains to the call to family, community, and participation. Herein, the discerning reader shall find an assemblage of key documents and encyclicals, each a testament to the Church's enduring wisdom and divine inspiration. Moreover, auxiliary resources for further study are meticulously curated to aid both the scholar and the devotee in their quest for a deeper understanding. Together, these hallowed writings form a compendium that both illuminates and fortifies the doctrines expounded in the preceding chapters, standing as both beacon and bastion for those who seek to propagate the Church's eternal truths and compassionate teachings.

Key Documents and Encyclicals

In the vast and intricate tapestry of Catholic Social Justice, certain documents and papal encyclicals stand out as the warp and weft that weave together a coherent and robust moral fabric. These writings encapsulate centuries of theological reflection, philosophical insight, and practical guidance aimed at fostering a just and harmonious society. Delving into these seminal texts, one encounters the heart and intellect of the Church's magisterium, as it speaks to the timeless principles of family, community, and participation.

Consider, for instance, the encyclical "Rerum Novarum," penned by Pope Leo XIII in 1891. This groundbreaking document addressed the pressing social issues of its time—the rise of industrial capitalism, the plight of the working class, and the responsibilities of employers. Beyond its historical context, "Rerum Novarum" lays the foundation for the Church's stance on social justice, emphasizing the dignity of labor, the rights of workers, and the necessity of solidarity and subsidiarity. Its echoes are found resonating through subsequent social encyclicals, proving its enduring relevance.

Fast forward to 1931, and Pope Pius XI's "Quadragesimo Anno," issued to mark the fortieth anniversary of "Rerum Novarum." This encyclical not only reaffirms Leo XIII's teachings but also delves deeper into the concept of social order. Pius XI speaks against the extremes of both capitalism and socialism, advocating instead for a balanced approach rooted in the principles of justice and charity. He elaborates on the idea of social reconstruction, emphasizing the need for structures that support the common good while respecting the autonomy of individuals and smaller communities.

The social teachings of the Church further evolved with Pope John XXIII's "Mater et Magistra" in 1961 and "Pacem in Terris" in 1963. "Mater et Magistra" expands on the themes of economic justice and social welfare, urging a more equitable distribution of resources and opportunities. "Pacem in Terris," on the other hand, is a clarion call for peace and human rights, addressing global issues such as disarmament, international relations, and the role of the United Nations. John XXIII's vision is one of global solidarity, transcending national boundaries to embrace the universal brotherhood of humanity.

Pope Paul VI continued this trajectory with his 1967 encyclical "Populorum Progressio," which can be seen as a manifesto for human development. Paul VI emphasizes that true progress is not measured solely by economic growth but by the holistic development of individuals and societies. He calls for international cooperation to address poverty, inequality, and social injustice, framing development as a moral imperative rooted in the dignity of the human person. His 1971 document "Octogesima Adveniens" further elaborates on these themes, urging local churches to engage actively with the specific social challenges of their contexts.

In more recent times, Pope John Paul II's extensive contributions to Catholic social teaching cannot be overlooked. His trilogy of social encyclicals—"Laborem Exercens" (1981), "Sollicitudo Rei Socialis" (1987), and "Centesimus Annus" (1991)—address a wide range of social issues, from the dignity of work and the option for the poor, to the challenges of globalization. John Paul II's philosophical depth and personalist perspective infuse these documents with a profound sense of moral urgency and spiritual vision.

Pope Benedict XVI's "Caritas in Veritate" (2009) takes up the mantle of his predecessors, exploring the relationship between charity and truth. Benedict XVI emphasizes that authentic human development requires a commitment to truth, which grounds and guides our efforts in love and justice. His reflections on the ethical dimensions of economic and technological progress call for a renewed sense of responsibility and stewardship in an interconnected world.

Pope Francis, currently shepherding the Church into the 21st century, has made significant contributions through his encyclicals "Laudato Si'" (2015) and "Fratelli Tutti" (2020). "Laudato Si'" is a groundbreaking document that addresses the ecological crisis, emphasizing our responsibility to care for creation and promoting an integral ecology that connects environmental, social, and economic dimensions. "Fratelli Tutti" is a poignant reflection on fraternity and social friendship, urging us to build a world where all people recognize each other as brothers and sisters, transcending divisions and conflicts.

The Church's social encyclicals are, in essence, a dialogue between faith and the world, grounded in the gospel values of love, justice, and peace. Each document builds upon the insights and teachings of its predecessors, creating a rich and dynamic body of social doctrine that speaks to the complexities and challenges of each epoch. These texts are not mere historical artifacts; they are living documents that continue to inspire and guide the faithful in their pursuit of a just and compassionate society.

The importance of these key documents and encyclicals in the context of Catholic social justice cannot be overstated. They provide a comprehensive and cohesive framework for understanding and addressing the social, economic, and political issues of our time. They call us to a higher standard of moral responsibility, urging us to transform our personal and communal lives in accordance with the principles of human dignity, solidarity, and the common good.

As we engage with these texts, we are invited to deepen our understanding of the Church's teachings and to discern how they apply to the specific circumstances and challenges we face today. This process of reflection and action is at the heart of Catholic social justice, which is not a static body of doctrine but a dynamic and evolving tradition that seeks to bring the light of the gospel to bear on the realities of our world.

In conclusion, the key documents and encyclicals of the Church articulate a vision of social justice that is deeply rooted in the gospel and the Church's rich theological and philosophical tradition. They challenge us to build a world that reflects the values of the kingdom of God—a world where all people can flourish and live in dignity, solidarity, and peace. As we strive to live out this vision in our families, communities, and societies, we are participating in the great work of redemption and the realization of God's plan for humanity.

Additional Resources for Further Study

To fathom the depths and intricacies of Catholic Social Justice fully, it is prudent to delve beyond the primary texts. The Church's doctrinal richness and extensive tradition offer a veritable cornucopia of literature and teachings for the enlightened mind eager to explore further.

Foremost among these resources are the encyclicals of various Popes. Encyclicals such as "Rerum Novarum," "Quadragesimo Anno," and "Caritas in Veritate" serve as cornerstone documents that encapsulate the Church's stance on social justice matters. These papal letters offer profound insights into the socio-economic and moral imperatives mandated by Catholic teaching.

Alongside these papal encyclicals, the compendia of Church Councils, notably the Second Vatican Council's "Gaudium et Spes," carry significant weight. This pastoral constitution is pivotal in understanding how the Church positions itself in relation to contemporary societal norms and challenges.

For those inclined towards a more theological exploration, the writings of the Church Fathers such as Augustine of Hippo, Thomas Aquinas, and John Chrysostom are indispensable. Augustine's "City of God" and Aquinas' "Summa Theologica" provide a foundational understanding of the philosophical and theological underpinnings of Catholic doctrine. Chrysostom's oratory skill and his elucidation of Christian morals afford timeless guidance on the application of social justice.

Amidst this theological tapestry, let us not overlook the importance of contemporary scholarship. Authors like Joseph Ratzinger, later Pope Benedict XVI, offer modern perspectives that harmonize age-old doctrine with the vicissitudes of the current age. His discourse in "Deus Caritas Est" seamlessly bridges doctrinal heritage and present-day praxis.

One must also consider the valuable contributions from Catholic Social Teaching (CST) resources. Among these, the "Compendium of the Social Doctrine of the Church" is paramount. This compendium serves as an extensive reference that delineates the principles of CST in a coherent and accessible manner.

Within the sphere of philosophical and sociological insights, the works of Étienne Gilson and Jacques Maritain stand out for their robust engagement with Catholic thought. Gilson's "The Spirit of Medieval Philosophy" meticulously articulates the medieval synthesis of faith and reason, while Maritain's "Integral Humanism" profoundly explores the nature of human dignity and society.

Psychological perspectives are not to be marginalized. The contributions of Viktor Frankl, especially in "Man's Search for Meaning," although not exclusively Catholic, resonate with the Church's understanding of suffering, purpose, and resilience. His existential analysis complements Catholic thought on human dignity and the search for transcendental meaning.

Moreover, practical guides for lay Catholics and pastoral workers are meritorious. Documents such as "The Vocation of the Business Leader" provide pragmatic approaches to integrating Catholic social principles in professional and personal spheres.

For those engaged in academic pursuits or wishing to deepen their scholarly engagement, journals like "Theological Studies," "Communio," and "The Review of Metaphysics" are invaluable. These journals offer peer-reviewed articles that span a breadth of topics from doctrinal theology to the intersections of faith and reason.

Furthermore, digital resources and online databases such as JSTOR, ATLA Religion Database, and the Vatican's own website offer easy access to a plethora of articles, papal documents, and theological dissertations. These platforms enable researchers to delve into primary sources and recent academic contributions to Catholic thought.

Educational institutions, especially those affiliated with the Church, regularly publish expansive and in-depth material. Universities like the Pontifical Gregorian University and the University of Notre Dame offer specialized courses, conferences, and publications that cater to those devoted to Catholic social justice and apologetics.

For those who seek community dialogue and broader perspective, Catholic social justice networks and organizations like Caritas Internationalis, the Catholic Worker Movement, and the Center for Concern provide resources that bridge theory and practice. Engaging with these organizations can offer practical insights and collaborative opportunities to enact social justice principles.

Finally, it is imperative to glean wisdom from lived experiences and historical precedents. Biographies and autobiographies of saints, social reformers, and contemporary Catholic leaders such as Dorothy Day, St. Teresa of Calcutta, and Oscar Romero illuminate how the principles of Catholic social justice are incarnated in everyday life and extraordinary circumstances.

To sum up, the additional resources for a profound understanding of Catholic social justice and apologetics range from ancient texts to modern interpretations, scholarly articles to practical guides, digital databases to community networks. This amalgamation equips the earnest seeker with the necessary tools to traverse the rich landscape of Catholic teachings, embodying the virtues of family, community, and participation in their fullest measure.